CONTENTS

29021

Gorseinon College
Learning Resource Centre
Belgrave Road : Gorseinon : Swansea : SA4 6RD Tel: (01792) 890731
This book is **YOUR RESPONSIBILITY** and is due for return/renewal
on or before the last date shown. 29021

CLASS NO. 823.914 ISH **ACC. NO.**

RETURN OR RENEW - DON'T PAY FINES

 Longman

 York Press

Sarah Peters is hereby identified as author of this work in accordance with Section 77 of the Copyright, Designs and Patents Act 1988

The author wishes to thank Faber and Faber Limited, for permission to reproduce extracts from *The Remains of the Day* by Kazuo Ishiguro

YORK PRESS
322 Old Brompton Road, London SW5 9JH

PEARSON EDUCATION LIMITED
Edinburgh Gate, Harlow,
Essex CM20 2JE, United Kingdom
Associated companies, branches and representatives throughout the world

First published 2000
Second impression 2001

ISBN 0-582-42462-3

Designed by Vicki Pacey
Phototypeset by Gem Graphics, Trenance, Mawgan Porth, Cornwall
Colour reproduction and film output by Spectrum Colour
Produced by Pearson Education North Asia Limited, Hong Kong

PART ONE

INTRODUCTION

HOW TO STUDY A NOVEL

Studying a novel on your own requires self-discipline and a carefully thought-out work plan in order to be effective.

- You will need to read the novel more than once. Start by reading it quickly for pleasure, then read it slowly and thoroughly.
- On your second reading make detailed notes on the plot, characters and themes of the novel. Further readings will generate new ideas and help you to memorise the details of the story.
- Some of the characters will develop as the plot unfolds. How do your responses towards them change during the course of the novel?
- Think about how the novel is narrated. From whose point of view are events described?
- A novel may or may not present events chronologically: the time-scheme may be a key to its structure and organisation.
- What part do the settings play in the novel?
- Are words, images or incidents repeated so as to give the work a pattern? Do such patterns help you to understand the novel's themes?
- Identify what styles of language are used in the novel.
- What is the effect of the novel's ending? Is the action completed and closed, or left incomplete and open?
- Does the novel present a moral and just world?
- Cite exact sources for all quotations, whether from the text itself or from critical commentaries. Wherever possible find your own examples from the novel to back up your opinions.
- Always express your ideas in your own words.

This York Note offers an introduction to *The Remains of the Day* and cannot substitute for close reading of the text and the study of secondary sources.

The Remains of the Day can be read on several different levels. It is a travel diary, an **elegy** to a lost era, an account of a wasted life and a love story about missed opportunities. It is the story of Stevens, a devoted butler, who takes a **literal** and **metaphorical** journey: he drives to Cornwall, but he also comes to examine his own existence, his values and his soul, and he faces the reality that is his life, which he has denied and repressed until now.

The story is set in the present of 1956 as Stevens drives towards Cornwall over several days. It contains memories, **flashbacks** and insights into the past that reveal Stevens's service to Lord Darlington. We learn how Stevens kept striving to attain the level of perfection he admires in butlers like his own father, and in his father's favourite story about the tiger under the table (see Summaries & Commentaries, Day One).

The novel works on a psychological level as Stevens and the reader gently probe Stevens's mind. Stevens is unable to analyse or be truly objective about events (until the very end), and this adds to the intrigue for the reader. The reader can see things that Stevens cannot, due to being sufficiently removed from the events, and the reader accompanies Stevens as he slowly faces the tragedies of his life. Kazuo Ishiguro captures Englishness, class, snobbery, fascism and naïveté in Stevens's **flashbacks** to the heyday of Darlington Hall and presents us with an English **anti-hero** in the form of Lord Darlington. He is at once everything that is great and everything that is not great about England: decent, honourable, repressed, modest, stubborn, old-fashioned. His compassion and outdated sense of fair play in the aftermath of the First World War, for the German people and, in particular, his friend Herr Bremann, lead him to Nazi sympathising and disgrace in the Second World War and afterwards (see Historical Background). Stevens mirrors this mixture of decency and gullibility: he serves Lord Darlington with a blind faith that chooses not to see his employer's faults, but eventually he must face the fact that he has wasted – and indeed sacrificed – his own life serving a man who was ultimately flawed and unworthy.

Kazuo Ishiguro presents Stevens's journey with a combination of **pathos** and restraint, provoking our compassion, frustration, respect and pity, as events move between comedy and tragedy. The richness of the narrative and the teasing way events unfold (see Narrative Techniques) provide us with pleasure, entertainment and – above all – a challenge, because things are not always as they seem. Readers must have their wits about them as they engage with this novel.

PART TWO

SUMMARIES & COMMENTARIES

The Remains of the Day was first published in hardback in 1989 by Faber and Faber. The paperback edition was first published in 1990. The 1996 Faber Library edition was used in the preparation of this Note.

SYNOPSIS

The novel is centred primarily around a motoring trip that the butler of Darlington Hall, Stevens, takes in 1956. Darlington Hall is now owned by an American, Mr Farraday. When Mr Farraday has to return temporarily to the United States, he offers Stevens the use of his Ford car, for a break, and Stevens plans to visit a former employee, Miss Kenton. This is misconstrued by Farraday, to the dismay of Stevens, who insists to the reader that he has a 'professional' motive only. The misunderstanding serves to highlight the apparent differences between English custom and American ways, and it becomes clear that Darlington Hall was in its heyday when it had a large staff under the late Lord Darlington, whom Stevens still reveres. As Stevens is the **narrator**, the reader is in no position to dispute his word (although he does reiterate his point about his 'professional' interest in Miss Kenton to a suspicious degree). As the novel unfolds, however, Stevens proves himself to be an unreliable narrator at times. He conveniently forgets things and unwittingly betrays himself later, and due to his inability to analyse events or people, he misses the glaringly obvious. The plot is framed by the motoring trip to Cornwall – hence the novel is divided into eight parts, covering the various stages of the journey, including the Prologue, where Stevens is at pains to explain himself. He is operating the Hall on a skeleton staff; he has given himself too much to do in his faulty staff plan and the return of Miss Kenton, who appears to be unhappily married, would solve this problem to some extent.

When Stevens sets off on his journey, we are given some detail and description of the places he stays in and visits, but dominating the narrative are Stevens's memories of the past, triggered initially by his review of the first day's travel, including an encounter with an old man on his way to Salisbury. This fuels the ongoing discussion within the novel about what constitutes a 'great' butler. Stevens arrives in Salisbury and remembers the arrival of his father and Miss Kenton at Darlington Hall, and his battle of wills with Miss Kenton. In the flashback she is fiery and stands up to Stevens, to his annoyance, but their animosity subsides when the increasingly frail Stevens senior falls over and goes into a decline, before dying of a stroke during an important international conference at Darlington Hall in 1923. Stevens feels he cannot leave his post to attend to his father, and a compassionate Miss Kenton steps in to do so. Prior to and during the conference, Lord Darlington's concern for the plight of Germany under the Treaty of Versailles is revealed, as well as his intention to help Germany.

Continuing on his car journey, Stevens is hampered by a lack of water in the car and he meets a chauffeur of a nearby house, who recognises him as being a servant and urges Stevens to visit Mortimer's Pond, a nearby beauty spot. While talking to the chauffeur, Stevens denies working for Lord Darlington. When at the pond, Stevens remembers doing the same in the presence of an American couple, the Wakefields, to Mr Farraday's annoyance. Later, at the Coach and Horses inn near Taunton, Stevens tries to banter with some of the locals, but is unsuccessful. The following morning, in a tea room in Taunton, he remembers the German Ambassador, Herr Ribbentrop, visiting Darlington Hall, but denies that Lord Darlington was ever anti-Semitic.

In the attic room of a cottage in Moscombe where he is staying the night, Stevens recalls why his lordship might have been labelled anti-Semitic: he sacked two maids because they were Jewish. There is a flashback to this event. Miss Kenton is outraged at Lord Darlington's actions but Stevens accepts his employer's wishes. Later on, Stevens insists to her that he was upset about it, but in his present-day narrative he maintains that it was a trivial and insignificant episode. A maid called Lisa replaces one of the dismissed employees. She appears unsuitable, but Miss Kenton insists that she be employed and endeavours to make a success of her, only to be disappointed when she runs away to marry the second footman. One day Miss Kenton goes into Stevens's pantry uninvited with flowers and finds him reading a romantic novel; Stevens is extremely uncomfortable and asks her to leave. Meanwhile, Miss Kenton begins to receive letters and becomes moody, which a colleague of Stevens, Mr Graham, explains is a sign of her wanting a family. Stevens dismisses this, although it transpires that she does have a 'suitor'. Earlier, in the summerhouse, Miss Kenton had provided Stevens with an opportunity to declare any feelings he might have, but he has insisted that Lord Darlington is the focus of his life, thus rejecting her. She loses her enthusiasm for their cocoa evenings which have been taking place recently and Stevens decides to end them altogether. His last memory of her at this time is when her aunt dies. She is crying in her room and he hesitates outside her door. He intends to express his condolences, but instead criticises her work.

Returning to the present day, Stevens explains that the car has run out of petrol, so he had to walk in the dark to a nearby village (Moscombe), where he met Mr Taylor, who offered him a room (where Stevens is currently writing). Mrs Taylor provides a meal and during the evening Stevens is mistaken for a genuine gentleman, which he goes along with, until it is apparent that a guest, Dr Carlisle, suspects he is an impostor. The discussion at the meal-table centred around politics, especially the views of the Taylors' neighbour, Harry Smith, and this provided Stevens with the chance to say he had met Winston Churchill and other leading politicians, which is, essentially, true. Continuing his **narrative** in the Taylors' attic room, Stevens remembers once being called into the drawing room at Darlington Hall and being questioned about politics by Mr Spencer. Stevens declined to reply; Mr Spencer and Lord Darlington laughed at him cruelly. Stevens distances himself from Lord Darlington's fascist views, explaining that it was nothing to do with him.

The following afternoon, at the Rose Garden Hotel in Little Compton, while waiting for his meeting with Miss Kenton, Stevens reveals that Dr Carlisle did guess he was a servant, and he also told Stevens of his own socialist beliefs. He helped Stevens to get some petrol, enabling Stevens to proceed with the journey. At the hotel, Stevens recalls an evening in 1936 when Mr Reginald Cardinal appears at the Hall uninvited, while the Prime Minister, the Foreign Secretary and Herr

Ribbentrop have secret talks, and Miss Kenton announces that she has had a proposal of marriage from her 'suitor', Mr Benn. Stevens gives little response to Miss Kenton's news so she goes out to meet Mr Benn and accepts his proposal. Stevens's focus is on providing excellent service for Lord Darlington's important meeting, and although a drunken Mr Cardinal tells him that Lord Darlington is gravely mistaken in his political views, to the point of being used by the Nazis for their own ends, Stevens refuses to listen. He remembers that it was on this night, not when Miss Kenton's aunt died, that he stood outside her room, briefly, aware that Miss Kenton was crying.

In Weymouth, towards the close of Stevens's **narrative**, he is sitting on a bench on the pier, waiting for the lights to be switched on. He recalls his meeting with Miss Kenton (now in fact Mrs Benn) in another **flashback**. She comes to the hotel and they talk for about two hours. He tells her about Lord Darlington's ruin, Mr Cardinal's death and his new employer, Mr Farraday. She tells him that her husband is to take early retirement through ill health and that her married daughter is expecting a baby. He drives her to the bus stop and asks her about the fact that she has left her husband on more than one occasion. She explains that he is a good man, whom she has grown to love. Yet sometimes she also thinks she has made a serious mistake with her life and she thinks about a life she might have had with Stevens. Stevens is heart-broken but he does not allow her to see it. She gets on the bus and they say goodbye.

On the pier in Weymouth, a retired butler chats to Stevens. Stevens reveals to him what a waste his life has been and that he has no dignity. He cries, but the man offers him hope, encouraging him to put the past behind him and to look forward to his old age, to enjoy the remains of his day. The man leaves, the pier lights come on and Stevens begins to think about the man's words. He starts to accept the past. He realises the true value of banter as he listens to the chatter of the people around him and plans to practise banter more wholeheartedly so that he can surprise Mr Farraday when he returns from America.

PROLOGUE: JULY 1956 (DARLINGTON HALL)

> **Stevens plans to visit Miss Kenton, a former employee of Darlington Hall, where he works as a butler. His new employer, the American Mr Farraday, has offered him the loan of his car**

The narrator, Stevens, tells us about a journey he is considering undertaking and informs us that he is the butler of Darlington Hall. He explains that the new American owner, Mr Farraday, has offered him the use of his car for a short break while he is in the United States for five weeks. Stevens is planning to visit a Miss Kenton who has recently written to him. She is a former employee of the Hall, who left in 1936 and now lives in Cornwall. Given the apparent break-up of her marriage, Stevens feels that she might be persuaded to return to work at Darlington Hall and thus help solve the problems he is currently experiencing with too few staff. Stevens explains that he has drafted a faulty staff rota in which he has given himself too much to do. He emphasises his 'professional' interest in Miss Kenton and is appalled at Farraday's misunderstanding of their relationship, as well as the inappropriateness of his employer's mode of expression. By the end of the Prologue, Stevens is resolved to make the planned journey.

> During these preliminary explanations, several themes are introduced. We learn that Darlington Hall was once a great house, needing a staff of between seventeen and twenty-eight people to run it, whereas now there are only four; we are told that Lord Darlington, the former owner, was a true 'English Gentleman' who always behaved appropriately, unlike the American, Mr Farraday; and we gain a sense of Stevens's nostalgia for the glorious past (see Critical Approaches on Themes). Farraday has tried to engage Stevens in 'banter' – casual and often humorous conversations that enable people, even strangers, to reach out and communicate with each other. This is a key theme that contributes to the unity of the plot. Stevens disapproves of banter, but feels it is his duty to participate, for his employer. His effort to engage Farraday in witty banter over the 'crowing noise' one morning is noticeable because of its failure.

Stevens's style of narration reveals much about his personality (see Narrative Techniques). He is a perfectionist and is careful to recall details, even trivial ones, to the point of seeming pedantic. His diction is archaic: he uses vocabulary such as 'partake of' rather than 'eat' and 'costume' rather than 'clothes'. His concern over the appropriate clothing for such a journey is a sign of his perfectionism and of the fact that he takes his position as butler and representative of Darlington Hall seriously; it also serves to introduce the imagery of clothes and appearances (see Imagery & Symbolism). Stevens takes the position of butler so seriously that he calls it a 'profession'.

chaise-longue a long couch-like chair for reclining

profession an occupation which requires advanced training in the liberal arts or sciences – for example, medicine, law or theology

fracas noisy argument

vocation a calling to a career, especially a religious one

valet a manservant whose duties involve looking after his employer's clothes and serving meals

Day one – evening (Salisbury)

Writing at a guest house, Stevens reflects upon his journey to Salisbury that day. He saw a marvellous view, which prompts him to consider England, Englishness and what constitutes a 'great' butler

At the end of the first day of his journey, Stevens has retired to his room in a guesthouse in Salisbury. He begins to go over the day's events starting with his reaction to leaving Darlington Hall. He goes on to describe an encounter with an old man who told him to climb a nearby hill to see a marvellous view. We then return to the guest house, and the landlady's reaction to Stevens's 'gentlemanly' demeanour is described. He explains that he departed on foot to explore Salisbury just after four o'clock that afternoon. This brings Stevens back to the earlier experience of the 'marvellous view', and the memory of it leads him to reflect on the English landscape and how English people mirror its calmness and restraint. This leads him to remember the debate he enjoyed in the past with his peers about 'what is a "great" butler?' He recalls various names and how they were lauded for their abilities and perhaps even admitted into the 'Hayes Society'. He explains that this was a club for excellent butlers only, run on the same lines as an exclusive Gentlemen's Club. The Hayes Society's criteria for membership required that the applicant worked for a 'distinguished household' and was 'possessed of a dignity in keeping with his position'. Stevens weighs up the concept of dignity and firmly believes it is something that one can learn rather than only be born with. He cites his own father, whom he trained under as a footman, as an example of this appropriate dignity. Stevens's father often recounted the tale of a butler in India who encountered a tiger under the dining table, a story which was the key to his outlook on his life and work. Stevens recalls how on one occasion his father dealt with three drunken gentlemen with dignity, and on another occasion acted as valet to 'the General' whose incompetence had caused the death of Stevens's elder brother, Leonard, during the South African War. The General is greatly impressed by Stevens senior and never knows of the private heartache he caused. Stevens concludes his ponderings with the certainty that it is Englishmen only who are capable of this 'dignity' and who make perfect butlers.

> The opening paragraph conveys a sense of ownership of Darlington Hall as Stevens is the last to leave and has to check the house over before he departs. He also feels 'odd' about leaving. He is not just leaving the Hall but the role of butler behind. Stevens has centred his whole life and identity on being a butler, so to be away from it is a big step (see Themes). This becomes more apparent as the **narrative** progresses.

> The meeting with the old man is the first of Stevens's encounters with ordinary people on a human level and it is not particularly successful. This and the subsequent encounters in the novel can be measured against one another to chart Stevens's progress with 'banter' and reaching out to people, as opposed to building barriers and shutting himself away (see Themes). Once he realises the man is not a 'vagrant', Stevens refers to him as 'some local fellow' who 'gave a rather vulgar laugh' and proceeds to address him inappropriately using vocabulary such as 'embarking' and

'somewhat premature' (p. 25). He even says, 'The fellow did not seem to understand me' but does not analyse why. Stevens has no sense of empathy – he is a snob and looks down on the man. Stevens could change to an appropriate **register**, not to patronise the man, but to be direct and understood; however, he does not do so. Yet the man urges him to see a view – this introduces an important theme into the novel (see also Themes). Stevens lacks self-awareness and cannot 'see' the reality that is his life. He also does not want to. The novel is in large part a psychological journey for Stevens as, during his trip, he remembers the past and begins to face facts and emotions he shut out at the time (see Imagery & Symbolism). 'Views' in the novel are closely connected with this idea: here, for example, Stevens is urged to 'see' a 'magnificent view', and in turn he 'sees' himself and his life. The old man gives him a warning, that he had better seize this opportunity to see the view before he is too old – this highlights the idea that time is running out for Stevens if he is to change or improve his life. He must destroy the barriers he has erected around himself and reach out to other people. Stevens takes the old man's advice and admits he is glad he made the effort to see the view. It gives him the 'frame of mind appropriate for the journey' and 'the first healthy flush of anticipation' (p. 26). He is helped and nourished by taking a break from journeying, both **literally** and **metaphorically**, although he reminds us once again that he has a 'professional' reason for the journey, in the form of Miss Kenton.

The theme of clothes and appearances emerges as Stevens allows himself to be received like a gentleman by the landlady. Stevens's explanation of the Hayes Society's 'distinguished household' criterion shows the snobbery underlying English society in general: it is clear that the club rejects butlers of wealthy people who have made their money, as opposed to those who have inherited it. The examples Stevens provides of 'dignity' reveal that a butler must be able to remain in the role of butler no matter what the circumstances. After a lengthy explanation of why his father was such a 'great' butler, citing examples of Stevens senior's inherent dignity, Stevens concludes that the very best butlers 'wear their professionalism as a decent gentleman will wear his suit' (p. 44). However, even whilst at the guest house, Stevens is unable to cease being a butler as he describes his room with a butler's eye, to the point that one can imagine him running his finger across surfaces looking for dust. He also sits on a 'hard-backed chair ... to await my tea' (p. 27). Stevens is on holiday, yet he is incapable of relaxing, and we begin to sense the extent to which he takes his job seriously. The personal and professional have collided and merged in his mind, making it impossible for him to 'switch off'.

The view he experienced remains with Stevens far more than the delights of Salisbury. In his room, he recalls its beauty and it leads him to reflect on England, its national character and its features. He feels England is great and that it is its 'calmness' and 'restraint', reflected in its people, that sets it apart from other countries. This passage lies at the heart of the theme of Englishness that centres around Lord Darlington and the code of decency and honour he lives by, that of gentlemanly behaviour (see Themes). This train of thought also leads Stevens to the topic of 'what is a "great" butler?' He creates a warm image of fellow butlers gathered around the fire in the evenings debating this very subject and he mentions a Mr Jack Neighbours. He explains that Jack Neighbours was hailed for a few years in the 1930s as being 'great' and, having said he has nothing against him, Stevens proceeds to dismiss him as little more than a flash in the pan. Stevens's true feelings about Jack Neighbours become evident later on. He goes on to cite another source for 'measuring' great butlers, the Hayes Society, and again his true feelings are repressed about the Society until a lot later on. There is much wrangling over this issue of greatness, until Stevens cites his father as a true example of greatness. Stevens reveals that he was trained by his father when he began his career as a footman. The two stories of absolute dignity on the part of Stevens's father, about the gentlemen's apology and the General, contrast markedly to the character of the father, whom we meet in the next chapter when he is past his prime. The 'tiger under the table' story also becomes a **metaphor** in the next chapter. It, too, highlights the degree of dignity and of appropriate behaviour expected in a butler, and how utterly a butler must become a butler rather than simply act like one – ideals to which Stevens has always aspired. This is the motivation behind Stevens's life, choices, attitude, language, values and persona. Unlike the butler in India, or his father, however, it would seem that Stevens has taken it too far. Stevens senior, whilst embodying the perfect butler, has not been too dignified to (presumably) get married and have two sons, although there is no mention of Mrs Stevens at all in the novel. Stevens, unlike his father, has never married and has denied himself love, marriage, a family and children.

Stevens starts to conclude his musings on the subject of the perfect butler with his own view of the matter, that 'one could recognize a great butler as such only after one had seen him perform under some severe test' (p. 44); this links the **narrative** neatly with Stevens's own great test recalled in the next chapter.

the Ritz and **the Dorchester** luxurious London hotels

National Geographic Magazine a popular magazine featuring articles and photographs from around the world

Bolshevik Russia a reference to the hard-line faction of the Marxist Russian Social Democratic Labour Party led by Lenin. The Bolsheviks believed in Communist doctrines based on the theories of Karl Marx. After the revolution in Russia broke out in February 1917 and the Tsar (Emperor) and his family were executed, Lenin's Bolsheviks overthrew the provisional government and seized power in October 1917. They established the first Soviet government and, as the Communist Party, became the only permitted political organisation in the USSR. By referring to the Bolsheviks, the members of the Hayes Society are suggesting that they should retain their essentially elitist structure rather than adopt a more open system as typified by Marxist ideals

falconing the art of keeping and training falcons

the Derby an annual horse race run at Epsom Downs in Surrey

a Memory Man at the music hall music halls provided live entertainment for the masses in the days before television. A Memory Man would entertain by astounding audiences with his ability to memorise vast quantities of facts at great speed

footman a male servant; a footman would often wear a uniform

industrialist someone who owns or controls a large number of factories or industrial enterprises

South African War a war between Dutch 'Boer' (farmer) settlers and the British Empire over diamond and gold deposits in South Africa (1899–1902); usually referred to as the Boer War, though it was in fact the second of two Boer Wars fought by the British (see also Chronology)

DAY TWO – MORNING (SALISBURY)

> **Stevens wakes up very early and re-reads Miss Kenton's letter, which causes him to recall their sometimes turbulent working relationship. Stevens describes how his father became ill and died at Darlington Hall, during an international conference in which Lord Darlington tried to promote moderation of the German reparation to the Allies**

The next morning, Stevens is wide awake and has shaved already, having had a poor night's sleep in a strange bed. It is too early for breakfast in the guest house, so he uses this time as an opportunity to go over Miss Kenton's letter again. He explains that 'Miss Kenton' is now Mrs Benn, having got married twenty years ago, in 1936. Stevens feels certain that her marriage is ending and her words cause him to remember a particular incident with his father at the Hall. Stevens recalls how his father and Miss Kenton arrived there at about the same time, in the spring of 1922. Stevens did not immediately get on with her and, by recounting five separate episodes in **flashback**, shows a marked battle of wills, ending in her victory when he is compelled to write a note and put it under her door in accordance with her wishes.

The focus of their sparring is Stevens's father. Although Stevens senior is employed at Darlington Hall as an under-butler, a position below that of Miss Kenton, Stevens insists Miss Kenton treat him as her superior, pointing out that she could learn a lot from him. She is very hurt by his words and over the coming weeks points out all the flaws in the work of the aged Stevens senior. At seventy-two, he is becoming increasingly infirm and one day falls over at the steps to the summerhouse. Stevens's father is relieved of his duties, at Lord Darlington's suggestion, and given lighter tasks to do.

In the midst of these, at times painful, memories, Stevens pulls back and recounts his day, how he drove towards Salisbury, narrowly avoided a chicken called Nellie, and enjoyed a splendid view of the cathedral spire. Returning to 1922, Stevens goes on to explain that the alarm over the summerhouse incident was also partly due to the fact that an unofficial international conference was due to be held at the Hall, and Lord Darlington and Stevens were particularly keen that it should proceed smoothly.

The conference involves key European diplomats and an American diplomat, Mr Lewis, arriving to discuss the plight of post-Great War Germany in the light of the Treaty of Versailles (see Historical Background). The French are keen to uphold the Treaty and Lord Darlington wants to try to persuade the French diplomat, referred to as M. Dupont (his real identity is not made explicit), otherwise. The diplomats assemble at the end of March 1923 and the conference begins. One of those gathered is Lord Darlington's friend Sir David Cardinal, whose son Reginald is due to be married soon. Stevens is entrusted with the task of explaining the facts of life to Reginald, but his attempts end in failure. Various discussions take place during the conference, including a tense debate on the final evening during which Mr Lewis (who is himself exposed as deceitful and scheming by M. Dupont) tells Lord Darlington that he is an 'amateur' at politics. At this time, Stevens's father is taken seriously ill and dies, but Stevens feels he cannot abandon his duties, especially to M. Dupont, whose feet are troubling him. In Salisbury, Stevens now prides himself on his dignity at such a difficult time.

> Stevens believes that Miss Kenton's marriage is at an end, which later proves to be not the case. However, at this stage this is not apparent and it is only later on in the novel that the reader's perspective on Stevens's interpretation changes. He also struggles to address her as Mrs Benn, a sign that he has not accepted her marriage. He talks of her loneliness and desolation, a life 'so dominated by a sense of waste' (p. 51), but by the end of the novel,

it becomes clear that he is projecting his own repressed feelings and fears onto her, that he is in fact talking about himself.

The clashes between Miss Kenton and Stevens are typical of the 'English' behaviour Stevens has ruminated over (see also Themes): true feelings are repressed and hidden behind extreme politeness. However, through their arguments, and when Stevens's father is gravely ill, we see that Miss Kenton is a woman of spirit, who does show her feelings to some extent: anger, irritation, pain, sarcasm, kindness, compassion and tenderness. This theme of Englishness is compounded by Lord Darlington's sorrow at the plight of his friend Herr Bremann. Lord Darlington's sense of dignity and fair play are violated by the treatment the Germans are receiving after the First World War, and what later becomes sympathy for the Nazi cause is rooted in a sense of honour and gentlemanly behaviour.

Stevens's conversation with the young woman outside Salisbury is a more successful encounter with an 'ordinary person' than that with the old man in Day One and he feels uplifted by her pleasantness. His snobbery is temporarily absent and their exchange is a positive step towards Stevens's ability to 'banter' (see Themes). The recollection of this incident also allows Stevens to draw back mentally from an especially painful memory, that of his father's physical decline. It is generally understood that expressing one's emotions, such as sadness or grief, helps with the healing process. Stevens has not faced, perhaps has been unable to face, these memories before, as he has not dealt with them or allowed himself to grieve. Thus the memories are as painful and acute in 1956 as they were in 1923. He has buried them, but this journey to Cornwall has allowed them to come to the surface. Stevens recounts the experience and then draws back, the first step in the healing process (see Imagery & Symbolism).

The events surrounding the international conference merit particular attention. Kazuo Ishiguro builds tension around the event in the words of Lord Darlington and his friends before it occurs and this is mirrored by the tension below-stairs, with

Stevens visualising himself as planning in the way that 'a general might prepare for a battle' (p. 81). He feels the weight of responsibility for the smooth running of events and also feels that he is contributing to its success by being so meticulous and efficient. He is the alter-ego of Lord Darlington here, and this dualism is mirrored further by the tension and strained relationship with his father at this time. Stevens's role model, who trained him years ago, is in decline (his plight and the fact that he has to work at the age of seventy-two serve as a reminder to the modern reader of life before trade unions and pensions were widespread). His body is weak but his spirit is not broken. The exchanges between Stevens and his father are revealing. Stevens covers his discomfort in their distant relationship with a 'short laugh' (p. 67) and addresses him as 'Father' in the third person: 'I hope Father is not being kept awake by his arthritic troubles' (p. 67). He often uses the neutral term 'indeed' in these exchanges – something which, in this instance, is another way of hiding his feelings. The dialogue is stark and there is no attempt by Stevens to analyse it; yet Stevens spends almost twenty lines describing the banqueting hall (p. 102), before launching into a highly detailed account of the discussion that suggests he has memorised every word and every detail of the occasion. In contrast, his father's room is described merely as a 'prison cell' (p. 67), the very phrase Miss Kenton uses about Stevens's pantry on p. 174. His father looks at his hands, as Miss Kenton does later on in the novel when the maid, Lisa, runs off with the second footman (see Imagery & Symbolism). He says he hopes he has been a good father to his son, who neither confirms nor denies it, and his hands, the **symbol** of his life's work and achievement, are empty. He appears 'faintly irritated' by his hands (p. 101), perhaps seeing, too late, his cold relationship with his son as a failure.

Juxtaposed against these tensions is an element of comedy in the form of Stevens's attempts to tell Reginald Cardinal about the facts of life. Stevens fails humorously, and a misunderstanding about being a nature-lover ensues just as M. Dupont, the key delegate, arrives. Stevens springs out from behind a bush, startles

Mr Cardinal and says he will be 'to the point'. However, he is far from it and an obscure discussion on nature and geese, initiated presumably by the concept of 'the birds and the bees', ensues. Stevens, though, appears to be unable to see the humour in this situation.

During the conference, Stevens's father is taken ill and all the servants, including Miss Kenton, display their distress and upset as his condition deteriorates over the next two days, with the exception of Stevens. He allows his professional duty to take precedence over personal disaster. As his father is dying, Stevens is encountered administering tea and port, giving instructions to footmen and tending to M. Dupont's feet. These are trivial tasks that could easily have been performed by someone else, but Stevens chooses to believe that he is indispensable. These trivialities have a larger significance (see Themes) and we see here another instance of Stevens and his inaccurate memory when he muddles Miss Kenton (pp. 61–2) and Lord Darlington (p. 63) as the speaker of the very words 'you must yourself realize their larger significance'. Trivialities hide, and distract Stevens from, the bigger issues in life – on this occasion death. Dupont is in physical pain and demands and receives alleviation for it, whereas Stevens is in emotional pain and represses it. There is a deliberate parallel here. Stevens has his 'duty' mixed up: his father is dying upstairs and Dupont has sore feet, yet he chooses to attend to Dupont. It can be argued, though, that Stevens cannot face this sorrow and uses his work as a means of escape.

Throughout these events, Miss Kenton is strong, kind, non-judgemental and tender. She comes across in a quiet way as being heroic. Stevens meanwhile shows a staggering restraint. This is his 'tiger under the table'. Unlike the butler in the story, however, who has a short-term situation to deal with, Stevens has a two-day struggle to contain and hide his turbulent feelings about the demise of his own father. He almost does not succeed.

Lord Darlington has invited Dupont to the conference with the intention of trying to soften France's rigid stance over the treatment of Germany. The American, Mr Lewis, feels that Dupont has not understood this and seeks him out to tell him so, and also to foil Lord Darlington's scheme. At the final dinner, Dupont reveals this to the entire delegation in a blunt and insulting speech directed against Lewis. Perhaps Dupont himself feels insulted at being thought gullible by Lewis. The speech is very 'un-English'. It is angry, attacking and hostile. Lord Darlington has also felt angry at Lewis, as Stevens indicates, but hides his feelings and remains 'a perfect gentleman', even when Lewis, who is far from humiliated, makes a speech of his own and calls Lord Darlington an 'amateur' at politics. The sad truth, however, is that Lewis is right. What Lewis sees and tries to articulate here is that post-First World War society is changing, breaking away from the traditions and codes of the nineteenth century. These are the codes that Lord Darlington adheres to, and he also expects everyone else to adhere to them too: decency, honour, duty, gallantry, fair play. The reader has the gift of hindsight, and can see what all of the delegates could never have foreseen: the world economic slump in the 1930s that worsened the already ailing Germany's plight and aided Adolf Hitler's rise in Germany. Hitler's systematic and brutal methods of seizing and maintaining power are totally at odds with Lord Darlington's values.

Kazuo Ishiguro offers an immediate example of this shift in codes and values, in the form of Dr Meredith. His grudging visit to Stevens's father and later non-appearance as he is dying show at once that not everyone conforms to these codes. Stevens's father is neither young, rich nor eminent and therefore Dr Meredith is dismissive of him. He prefers, perhaps, to finish his dinner and enjoy port and cigars of his own, rather than administer relief to a poor old man who will be dead soon anyway. When he finally arrives after Stevens's father has died, he only stays for a few minutes, but attends to the 'distinguished' Dupont's feet without hesitation. The precedence he shows Dupont over Stevens's father parallels that of Stevens himself, but is motivated by very different reasons.

As the conference is ending, with apparent success for Lord Darlington, Stevens receives the news of his father's death from Miss Kenton in another staggering display of restraint, which could leave the reader thinking that Stevens is cold and inhuman; yet he has already given himself away. Continuing the theme of seeing, Mr Cardinal and Lord Darlington see the distress on Stevens's face. He is crying as he serves the port and they are the only ones to notice. The others, like Dupont, see Stevens as a mere functionary, although Stevens does receive his 'reward': this is the praise he receives from Dupont and the German countess for excellent service, which is reminiscent of his father's encounter with the General recounted in the previous chapter. Comedy punctuates the tragedy of Stevens senior's death with the reappearance of Mr Cardinal. The absurdity of these 'niceties' is apparent to the modern reader. They are bound by class, though, and the codes and rituals embedded in the class system. Stevens is unaware of all of this and he does not attempt to analyse anything except what makes a 'great' butler. He contents himself at the end of the chapter by concluding that the events were a 'turning point' for him professionally and he feels that, whilst not attaining 'greatness', he was somewhat dignified and he feels 'a large sense of triumph' over it. The discerning reader might well by now have ceased to be fooled by the excessive humility Stevens frequently expresses.

John Maynard Keynes (1883–1946) a British economist who acted as an adviser at the Versailles Peace Conference and was opposed to the economic terms of the Treaty. In 1919 he wrote *The Economic Consequences of Peace*, in which he predicted that the reparations Germany was being forced to pay would result in increased nationalism and militarism. These predictions were correct

H. G. Wells Herbert George Wells (1866–1946) was an English author and political philosopher who was deeply interested in the survival of society. In addition to many works of fiction he wrote a very popular historical work, *The Outline of History*, in 1920

Mr Lloyd George David Lloyd George (1863–1945), First Earl of Dwyfor, was the British Prime Minister from 1916 to 1922. After the 1918 armistice he took part in the peace conference and helped to draw up the Treaty of Versailles

the Versailles treaty the Treaty of Versailles was the peace treaty between Germany and the Allies which was signed on 28 June 1919 at the Palace of Versailles, near Paris. It forced Germany to abolish compulsory military service, reduce its army to 100,000, demilitarise certain territories around the Rhine River, cease production and trade of war materials, cut back drastically on its navy, and abandon aviation except for domestic purposes. On top of this, reparation payments had to be made

German reparation payments part of the Treaty of Versailles stipulated that Germany had to 'pay back' the Allies for the damage they had incurred during the First World War. The reparations included money and also ships, trains, livestock and natural resources

the Ruhr the name of a river and a region in Germany. The area is one of the most intensely developed industrial regions in the world, because of the coal deposits there. The development of coal mining and heavy industry in the Ruhr began in the nineteenth century and it became the core of the German war effort in both World Wars

Day two – afternoon (mortimer's pond, dorset)

> Pausing en route at Mortimer's Pond, Stevens continues
> to reflect upon the question of 'what is a "great" butler?'.
> He remembers two occasions when he denied working for
> Lord Darlington, but reiterates his faith in him and how
> proud he feels to have worked for him

Stevens picks up the thread of his discussion of 'what is a "great" butler?' whilst sitting on a bench beside Mortimer's Pond, a beauty spot. He does not reveal his whereabouts until pp. 126–7. He begins his discussion abruptly, asserting that he believes there to be a 'whole dimension to the question' which he has not yet considered. He explains that the Hayes Society's requirement that a member must be 'attached to a distinguished household' (p. 119, repeated from p. 32) is clearly out of date as it refers to the traditional distinction between old (inherited) and new (acquired through business) money. However, he concedes that the underlying principle is sound but that it depends on one's definition of 'distinguished'. Stevens asserts his belief in the 'moral' status of an employer, and in members of his profession's desire to serve 'gentlemen who were, so to speak, furthering the progress of humanity' (p. 120). He expands this idea by explaining that the old view of the world was in terms of a ladder, the concept of hierarchy. A more modern view, in his eyes, is that of a wheel which emanates political power and the closer one is to the hub, the closer one is to the power source. Stevens states that he himself changed jobs several times 'before being rewarded at last with the opportunity to serve Lord Darlington' (p. 122). He admits that he has never seen matters in this way before and feels that it has to do with events that occurred as he entered the Dorset region earlier in the day, which he then relates.

The car begins to smell, so he stops, but discerning danger in the situation, proceeds in the car to seek help and comes across the chauffeur to a colonel who owns a large Victorian house. The chauffeur explains that the car needs water and attends to it. During the conversation that ensues, he discovers that Stevens is from Darlington Hall and enquires about Lord Darlington. Stevens denies having ever worked for him. The chauffeur suggests that Stevens visits Mortimer's Pond, which he does.

Returning to the present, Stevens contemplates his actions in denying that he worked for Lord Darlington and feels he has displayed 'distinctly odd behaviour' (p. 128). He remembers that it is not the first time he has done this and describes what occurred when an American couple, the Wakefields, visited Darlington Hall and were given a tour. He was surprised by their architectural knowledge, and that of Mr Farraday, and recalls how he denied having ever worked for Lord Darlington when asked about it by Mrs Wakefield. Mr Farraday is annoyed by Stevens's denial, as he feels it made him look foolish and dishonest. Stevens gives him a convincing reason why he did so: he tells Mr Farraday that it is not the English way to discuss one's former employer.

Stevens then continues his **narrative** by protesting against all the 'foolish things' (p. 132) that are said about Lord Darlington. He asserts that his own behaviour could perhaps be explained as a way of discouraging hearing 'such nonsense concerning his lordship' so as to avoid unpleasantness. He proclaims Lord Darlington to have been 'a gentleman of great moral stature' among other things and claims that he himself did work 'as close to the hub of this world's wheel as one such as I could ever have dreamt', that he did work in a 'distinguished household'. He ends by stating how proud he is to have had this privilege.

The shifts in the **narrative** during this chapter come almost as a warning to the reader, a warning to be aware that the reader's perspective can be changed within a matter of pages. Such a change happens here when we are involved in Stevens's debate about 'great' butlers with no real idea of where exactly Stevens is. Suddenly we learn that he is actually sitting on a bench beside Mortimer's Pond. These shifts happen elsewhere in the novel in less obvious ways (see Narrative Techniques).

Stevens's encounter with the chauffeur is noteworthy as it is a pleasant, successful encounter, compared to the one with the old man, but it raises problems for Stevens in terms of admitting to his association with the apparently disgraced Lord Darlington. The reader does not yet know exactly what it is Lord Darlington has done and thus can only sympathise or accept Stevens's words at face value. Stevens faithfully recounts the conversation with the chauffeur, including the **colloquialisms** and **idioms** which, besides his job, mark him out as being working-class: 'hit the jackpot first time … guv … an old beauty like this … geezer' (pp. 124–5). They are in direct contrast to Stevens's formal vocabulary: 'promontory … pervades … sustaining damage to my travelling suit' (p. 127).

The Colonel's attempt to sell the Victorian house off is a reminder of the sale of Darlington Hall and the demise of Lord Darlington, and of the changing modern world in general, although this is not developed or analysed by Stevens. The reduced role of the man from batman to chauffeur, valet, butler and cleaner is an echo of Stevens's own reduced role at Darlington Hall. Stevens's denials of working for Lord Darlington are surprising, as Stevens has always spoken respectfully and admiringly of him; this causes the reader to suspect that Stevens is hiding his true feelings and deliberately being misleading. However, in fairness, he seems genuinely perplexed by his actions and his lack of self-awareness is so great that he is unaware of his true feelings, or cannot face them. These denials are in some ways reminiscent of Peter's denials of Christ after the Crucifixion, as told in the New Testament Book of Mark (see Imagery & Symbolism).

The denials are part of Stevens's mental journey. He has admitted to this 'distinctly odd behaviour', although he does not understand it. He has managed to link the incident with the chauffeur to the similar incident with the Wakefields, but he concludes his ponderings with an assertion of his devotion to Lord Darlington, a repression again of his true feelings. This is in stark contrast to the ending of the previous chapter, where he was speaking in a modest and humble tone about his own achievements – here he is proudly boasting that because Lord Darlington was great, he too attained greatness. He is not even above using Mr Farraday's ignorance about English ways to his own ends and deceiving him. Thus it becomes clear that Stevens's previous contempt for the Hayes Society is born of repressed anger, envy and frustration about the fact that, even had the Society continued to the present day, he would never have been a member precisely because of Lord Darlington, the man he has blindly devoted himself to. The distinction made between 'old' and 'new' money is significant because, in his prime, Stevens's father worked for Mr John Silvers, an industrialist whose money came from his business. It seems that Stevens's contempt for the Hayes Society is due to his father's exclusion from it as much as his own. This connects with Stevens's admiration for his father and the fact that he cites him as an example of being a great butler in Day One.

The last pages of this chapter thus cause a change of perspective as we no longer see the quiet, modest Stevens, but a proud, self-seeking man who is hiding his bitterness at the recognition he has always been denied, disguising his anger at the way he has been let down by Lord Darlington and revealing his frustration at having to bear the shame of Lord Darlington's disgrace. The tone of this passage on pp. 132–3 is increasingly angry and bitter and is in contrast to the humble and modest tone of the end of the previous chapter. At last, there is a glimpse of his true personality (see Narrative Techniques). Stevens is a human being after all, a flawed man with real emotions which he has successfully hidden and repressed for nearly all of his professional life. The modesty and humility he usually displays is not an act but a persona, a subconsciously created identity that Stevens uses to rid himself of his emotions and come closer to attaining perfect butler status. Kazuo Ishiguro has constructed the narrative in such a way that we feel it is doubtful and unlikely that Stevens realises he is doing this. There appears to be no malice in it. Stevens's use of this persona ties in with the motif of clothes, that clothes make a person a gentleman (see Imagery & Symbolism), just as language, idioms and colloquialisms reveal a person's class in the novel. Stevens 'puts on' his persona, his modest demeanour, like clothing, but occasionally, as when Mr Cardinal and Lord Darlington notice him crying, and here with his denials of working for Lord Darlington, cracks in his smooth exterior appear.

Stevens's surprise at the Wakefields' architectural knowledge and also that of Mr Farraday is a reminder of his suspicion, caution and apparent dislike of Americans (see Themes). The behaviour of Mr Lewis described in the previous chapter could be the source of this. Stevens's narration clearly shows him siding against Lewis with Lord Darlington and the others. He even tells Lord Darlington the details of an overheard conversation between Dupont and Lewis, to contribute to Lord Darlington's cause, and although it is never stated, one can only imagine his chagrin at Lewis's speech in which he attacks Lord Darlington and calls him an 'amateur'.

Stevens is sitting at Mortimer's Pond, having taken the chauffeur's advice to visit it. This is an echo of the old man who urges Stevens to see a fine view when he is on his way to Salisbury and, by taking time out from travelling, he is encouraged on many levels to continue (see Themes). It is important for Stevens to take time to reflect whilst on his mental journey, as it enables him to remember and examine the past and thus proceed to the future. Stevens sees events increasingly clearly when he takes time to enjoy a view. When he is on the hill in Day One, he 'sees' England and

Englishness, looking far into the distance to take stock of what it means to be English. Here, beside the pond, Stevens reflects upon himself as he looks over the water. The water acts as a **literal** and **metaphorical** mirror: although he is unable to analyse his behaviour, he sees himself and the cracks in his 'mask'. He is also concerned about dirtying or damaging his clothes which **symbolise** the outer persona he has created (see Imagery & Symbolism). Metaphorically, he does not want the 'outer' to be tainted or ruined by the 'inner', his hidden real self, which the pond reflects and reveals.

DAY THREE – MORNING (TAUNTON, SOMERSET)

Stevens describes the events of the previous evening, when he stayed at an inn near Taunton and unsuccessfully practised bantering with the locals. He also reflects upon the importance of silver polish, meetings between Lord Darlington and Herr Ribbentrop and his present problem of a faulty staff rota, with which he hopes Miss Kenton can assist

This chapter opens with a description of the events of the previous evening, when Stevens stayed overnight at the Coach and Horses inn near Taunton.

Having eaten a sandwich in his room, Stevens feels restless and decides to go into the bar to try some cider. He sits away from the locals, but they engage him in conversation and he attempts to banter with them. He is not successful and spends the rest of the night agonising about possible offence he might have caused and feeling disappointed because he has been practising banter in order to be better at it. In the morning it is clear that no offence was taken and he explores Taunton.

Stevens reveals that he is actually sitting in a tea room at this point in his **narrative** and he comments on the other people in the tea room. He also looks out of the window and sees a sign to the village of Mursden which he remembers is the place where the firm of Giffen and Co., the makers of excellent silver polish, was situated. This leads into a reverie on the importance of excellent silver polish. Stevens recalls how the silver at

Darlington Hall was much commented on by important visitors, such as Lord Halifax, when he was there for meetings with Herr Ribbentrop. Stevens explains that not only was Lord Darlington taken in by Ribbentrop, but many other important people were too, and he asserts that Lord Darlington was in no way anti-Semitic, apart from during one minor incident.

The narrative returns to the topic of silver and Stevens reiterates how it contributed to easing relations between Lord Halifax and Herr Ribbentrop. Stevens reasserts how satisfying it is to serve someone important who can 'further the cause of humanity' (p. 147), but then turns his mind to the present as he has 'many more years of service' left and he has been experiencing problems in the employment of Mr Farraday. These problems, apart from the faulty staff rota, as discussed in the Prologue, include sub-standard silver-polishing, it would seem, to Stevens's embarrassment. He reminds us that the return of Miss Kenton would help with this. He admits he re-read her letter whilst at the inn the previous night but is now struggling to find exactly where she states her desire to return to the Hall; but as he will see her within the next two days, he feels that there is no point in worrying unduly about this.

The Coach and Horses appears to be stereotypically 'olde worlde', with its thatch, timbers and local cider – Stevens seems to be immersed in a traditional, picture-book England like that portrayed in Mrs Symons's *The Wonder of England*, which he mentions in the Prologue. He states (p. 12) that of the illustrations in Mrs Symons's book, he prefers the artists' sketches (which are perhaps more liable to be subjective interpretations of English scenes) to the photographs (which are in some ways more objective and 'accurate' portrayals). This suggests that Stevens himself prefers to give a subjective, artistic view of traditional England rather than a more objective portrayal grounded in the present-day reality of 1956 (see Place & Time, and Themes on Englishness & Americans).

Stevens now appears to be relaxing at last. Instead of sitting on a hard-backed chair awaiting his tea as he did in Salisbury, he has a sandwich and feels restless to the point of venturing into the bar and even trying some cider. He sits apart from the locals and struggles to relate to them, reverting to his usual, neutral 'indeed', but this is a small and significant progression.

The theme of banter is resumed in this chapter with Stevens's failed attempt to engage with the locals, but at least he is trying to reach out to them. This is a change from the previously snooty and superior attitudes he has displayed so far towards ordinary people. From the agonising that follows, it is clear how seriously Stevens regards his 'duty' of bantering and also how seriously he takes himself. He has been 'studying' a witty radio programme and has devised a 'simple exercise' of trying to 'formulate three witticisms based on my immediate surroundings … Or … three witticisms based on the events of the past hour' (p. 139). Despite his efforts, it never occurs to him that it is the delivery of his witty remarks that is at fault, that because of this, he is just not funny. The locals in the bar are only able to tell he is trying to be witty when they notice the 'mirthful expression on my face' (p. 138) and thus we can infer that he delivered his witticism with his usual neutral tone of voice. He is unable to see this; nor is he aware of how humorous he seems by doing his 'simple exercise', just as he was unable to see the humour in his encounters with Mr Cardinal, because he was taking his duty too seriously. He resolves to cease trying to banter with Mr Farraday until he is better at it – again, taking his duty to excess. He certainly fails to see any humour in his encounter with Farraday over the tarnished fork, feeling embarrassed about it. It is not certain that Farraday was in fact unhappy with the fork, as he looks at it briefly in an absent-minded way, but Stevens interprets this as criticism and changes the fork. It is the manner in which he does so that appears to be humorous, as he startles Farraday twice. The silent misunderstanding and failure of communication in this incident, with Farraday merely reading the paper at breakfast and Stevens overanalysing his every movement or lack of movement, highlight the gulf between them. The incident also perhaps provides a clue to the reasons behind Stevens's endless pre-empting of criticism. He is continually justifying and explaining himself, as though to avoid criticism, and here it clearly centres around his employer. He feels himself to be under constant scrutiny and open to criticism, not just at international conferences, but during everyday events such as breakfast.

The signpost, which triggers the silver-polishing discussion, is a **metaphor** for Stevens finding his own emotional route as much as being a physical pointer. It suggests a focus on things rather than on people, silver objects rather than concern for other human beings, which is unsurprising considering Stevens always chooses his job over life's important issues (see also Imagery & Symbolism). These issues include family, death, love, marriage and children. In Day Two – Morning, for example, we saw that he chose his duty as a butler over the death of his father.

Stevens's **narrative** now causes unease as we can no longer be sure that we trust him as a **narrator** (see Narrative Techniques). The 'real' Stevens, a proud, angry, bitter man, was seen at the end of the last chapter. Here, when he mentions Mr Jack Neighbours in his discourse on silver polish, our perception has changed and his previous, more moderate, words about him need to be re-examined. Now, they seem specious and hollow. The reader has become aware of Stevens's hidden feelings and what they consist of, and can no longer take him at face value. Stevens is clearly jealous of, and bitter towards, Mr Jack Neighbours. He also shows a certain amount of arrogance, pride and vanity regarding his contribution to the smoothness of the meeting between Lord Halifax and Lord Darlington. He is adamant that he made an impact on Lord Darlington's success with Herr Ribbentrop and the Nazis, but fails to see that this also means he contributed to Lord Darlington's downfall when he is disgraced by it. Stevens reverts to his modest persona at this point, saying it was only a 'small factor' (p. 146), and he defends Lord Darlington for several pages over his connection with Herr Ribbentrop. He also thinks he is merely illustrating his points about silver polish, but he is actually revealing the extent of Lord Darlington's involvement with the Nazis and his meddling in politics. Stevens cannot see that he is telling us more than he perhaps intended to, nor can he see that the meeting was dangerous for England, due to his persistent blind faith in Lord Darlington (see also Themes). He neither saw it at the time, nor does he see it now, in 1956. He even describes Herr Ribbentrop, who was hanged for war crimes, as a 'trickster' (p. 144) − an understatement that connects to Stevens's excessive playing-down of Lord Darlington's 'sins'. There is **irony** evident in these passages since Stevens has earlier asserted that Lord Darlington served humanity, whereas clearly he did not. He fraternised with the Nazis and tried to manipulate the politics of the day, to the point of endangering England, the full extent of which is not yet revealed.

Stevens is also blind to the resonant words of the American Mr Lewis, which we see starting to come true. Perhaps, though, Stevens is not so blind to Lewis's words and simply chooses not to see them − perhaps it is the very fact that Stevens knows that Lewis was right which fosters his attitude of unease around the other American, Mr Farraday. Stevens also reveals more than he probably intends to with his words about Miss Kenton at the end of the chapter. It concludes with a poignant, tender image of him thinking about Miss Kenton and her letter as he is going to sleep at the Coach and Horses inn, and he betrays how much he needs her, misses her and loves her, although he is unable to admit this to himself. He lies there listening to the landlord and his wife clearing up, a parallel to his former relationship with Miss Kenton, when they worked side by side at Darlington Hall. It is also a reminder of what might have been.

Stevens's defence of Lord Darlington and assertion about others also welcoming Herr Ribbentrop into their midst is problematic, as we cannot be certain how true this actually is or how far we can trust Stevens's word at this point. It is also revealed in this chapter that Stevens has read into Miss Kenton's letter sentiments which were not there, which he admits were 'wishful thinking' on his part. This contradicts his words in Salisbury and further adds to our mistrust of his **narrative** (see Narrative Techniques).

Stevens retracts from painful memories about the past with the words 'But I drift' (p. 146) and then re-establishes emotional equilibrium with a small tirade against those who disagree with his point of view. He reveals how satisfied he feels in being able to show they are wrong. Further underlying **irony** is present here: he goes on to mention again the 'small errors' he spoke of in the Prologue and with the hindsight of the chapters about his father, it seems as though Stevens is worried about becoming like him in his own old age. Stevens is worried about looking into the past so much when he still has so many years of service ahead of him, a concept which is explored more fully at the end of the novel.

The question of who the intended audience for this 'travel diary' might be (see also Narrative Techniques) takes an interesting turn in this chapter, when Stevens writes: 'Perhaps "Mursden" will ring a bell for you' (p. 141). The reference to Mursden as the home of Giffen and Co. is expected to be grasped by a reader familiar with these things, although it could be argued that Stevens, so entrenched in his closed world and with such a narrow outlook, expects everyone to be familiar with them. However, the term 'our' as in 'our profession' (p. 142) is an inclusive one that clearly suggests that the reader is a fellow servant. Perhaps this is a posthumous document for his father, or intended for the butler he meets at the end of the novel.

Lady Astor Nancy Witcher Langhorne (1879–1964), Viscountess Astor, was born in Virginia, USA, and married Waldorf Astor, her second husband, in 1906. He served as a Member of Parliament from 1910 until 1919, when he entered the House of Lords as Viscount Astor. In the same year, Lady Astor was elected to the House of Commons. She was the first woman to hold a seat in Parliament and retired in 1945

Lord Halifax Edward Frederick Lindley Wood (1881–1959), First Earl of Halifax, was born at Powderham Castle in Devon (where the Merchant–Ivory film of *The Remains of the Day* was made). He was a member of the Conservative Party in the House of Commons between 1910 and 1925, before becoming Viceroy of India 1926–31. As Viceroy, he strove to end the unrest against the British government through a policy of co-operation with Indian nationalist leaders. He became the third Viscount Halifax in 1934 and Conservative Party leader in 1935. In 1938 he was appointed

D̲ay three – morning continued

Foreign Secretary and played an important role in the negotiation of the Munich Agreement signed on 29 September 1938. The Agreement, signed by Neville Chamberlain (the British Prime Minister), Edouard Daladier (the French Prime Minister), Adolf Hitler and Benito Mussolini, violated the Treaty of Versailles and allowed Germany to regain possession of the Sudetenland (part of Czechoslovakia)

Herr Ribbentrop Joachim von Ribbentrop (1893–1946) was born in Wesel, Germany, educated in France and England and served in the German army during the First World War. A wealthy wine merchant, he joined the Nazi Party in 1921 and served as Ambassador to Britain from 1936 to 1938. He negotiated the alliances known as the Rome–Berlin–Tokyo Axis, as well as the German–Soviet non-aggression pact of 1939. He also helped plan and execute the German programme of expansion which led to Austria and Czechoslovakia's annexation and culminated in the Second World War. He was hanged in 1946 after his arrest by British troops and conviction at the Nuremberg war crimes trials

British Union of Fascists a political organisation formed in 1932 by Sir Oswald Mosley. Their members were known as 'blackshirts' because of the colour of their uniforms. See also Historical Background

D̲ay three – evening (moscombe, near tavistock, devon)

Stevens is staying overnight with the Taylors, who have mistaken him for a genuine gentleman. He describes how two Jewish maids were sacked by Lord Darlington and replaced by Lisa, who later eloped with the second footman. He considers various reasons for the change in his relationship with Miss Kenton, discusses the concept of dignity and concludes by distancing himself from Lord Darlington and his mistakes

Stevens's **narrative** returns to Lord Darlington's attitude to 'Jewish persons'. He is adamant that Lord Darlington was not anti-Semitic except for during one 'brief, entirely insignificant' incident when he dismissed two maids because they were Jewish. Stevens goes on to explain that Lord Darlington was influenced by Mrs Carolyn Barnet, an English Nazi sympathiser and a member of the British Union of Fascists headed by Sir Oswald Mosley (see Historical Background).

One day, Lord Darlington summons Stevens and insists on the dismissal of two maids, Ruth and Sarah, because they are Jewish. Stevens accepts this and informs Miss Kenton, who is outraged and questions her employer's judgement, for which Stevens reprimands her. Miss Kenton declares it is a 'sin' to dismiss them, but Stevens cannot see or admit it. She vows she will leave but as the weeks go by, she remains at the Hall. About a year later, Lord Darlington admits he was wrong to dismiss the maids and seeks to atone for his actions. On meeting in the summerhouse, Stevens tells this to Miss Kenton, who admits she had planned to leave but stayed out of cowardice. Stevens confesses to being distressed by what happened the previous year and Miss Kenton is incredulous, as he had not revealed any of his feelings at the time. Indeed, she accuses him of always having to 'pretend'. Stevens denies that this is the case.

One of the replacements for Ruth and Sarah is a young woman called Lisa. Stevens feels she is unsuitable for the job – she has dubious references and left her last post in mysterious circumstances – but Miss Kenton insists that she be taken on despite Stevens's objections. Lisa thrives under Miss Kenton's care and instruction, to Miss Kenton's delight, but leaves abruptly about eight or nine months later with the second footman. They have run off together as they are in love and leave letters behind declaring this. Miss Kenton is upset and admits to Stevens that she was wrong. She is convinced that the young woman had a promising career in front of her and that she will ultimately regret the choice she has made.

In the present-day **narrative**, Stevens changes the subject to explain that he is staying overnight with a Mr and Mrs Taylor, in their small cottage. He goes on to explain that after being unable to find a room for the night in Tavistock, he proceeded to look for accommodation further afield, got lost and ran out of petrol. This resulted in his searching for assistance on foot, which led him to a village. He eventually came across Mr Taylor, who kindly offered him a room overnight. Stevens says that the events of the evening with the Taylors have been 'far more taxing' than his car problems. He then ponders the 'change' in his relationship with Miss Kenton during 1935–6, before she left the Hall, and feels that one particular encounter 'marked a crucial turning point'.

Miss Kenton has, a few times, brought flowers into Stevens's pantry, but on one occasion she discovers Stevens reading a book which he hides from her and which she insists on seeing. She advances and he retreats. As she is standing in front of him, the atmosphere in the room changes, and she leans in and prises the book from his grasp, while he looks away. She discovers and comments on the fact that it is only a romantic novel and he shows her out. He is then at great pains to explain to the reader that he was reading such a novel for professional purposes only and thus to enhance his vocabulary. He explains that he feels it is also important that Miss Kenton and other staff never see him 'off duty' and that following this episode, he resolves 'to set about re-establishing our professional relationship on a more proper basis'.

The present-day Stevens also feels that there may well have been other factors that contributed to the change in their relationship, factors such as Miss Kenton's days off. He describes how up until about a month before the encounter in the pantry, Miss Kenton had very few days off, except to see her aunt every six weeks. We also learn that Stevens has no days off.

Miss Kenton suddenly begins taking all her allocated time off. Stevens comments on this, and on her mood swings, to his colleague Mr Graham, who seems to be aware of what she is going through and predicts that she wants a husband and family, which Stevens strongly disputes. He does, however, start to wonder if she has a 'suitor', especially when she begins to receive regular letters with a local postmark. Feeling perturbed about her possible impending departure, Stevens raises this topic with her and she unburdens herself about her suitor, who used to be a butler, although not to Stevens's standard, but who now has his own business. She suggests that Stevens must be a well-contented man, but he refutes this by saying that only when Lord Darlington feels contented will he, Stevens, be able to feel that way too. Miss Kenton's mood changes and, soon afterwards, their evening meetings with cocoa come to an end – on one of these evenings Miss Kenton expresses how tired she feels and Stevens suggests that they cease them altogether.

Stevens now wonders how things might have turned out if he had behaved differently. At around the same time, Miss Kenton's aunt died. Stevens had wondered how to console her but ended up criticising her work and hurting her feelings instead. In the midst of telling us this,

Stevens abruptly changes the subject to recount the present evening's events with the Taylors. Having admitted that he now realises that he has read too much into Miss Kenton's letter, he goes on to describe how the Taylors and their neighbours, who visited that evening, mistook Stevens for a genuine gentleman. He played along with this, but when Dr Carlisle, one of the visitors, arrived and fixed his gaze upon him, Stevens became uncomfortable and retired to bed. Stevens still feels very uncomfortable about what has happened and thinks about what Mr Harry Smith, another of the visitors, said about dignity. This causes Stevens to recall an episode when, around 1935, Lord Darlington summoned him to be asked questions on current events by a guest named Mr Spencer. Stevens declined to answer the questions and Mr Spencer humiliated and mocked him, actions for which Lord Darlington apologised the next day. Stevens describes how Lord Darlington had aged physically and how Lord Darlington tried to justify Mr Spencer's treatment of Stevens. Lord Darlington also expressed his own fascist and anti-democratic views to Stevens, who reiterated his opinion that it is his place as a butler merely to provide 'good service'. On the strength of this recollection, Stevens dismisses Harry Smith's democratic views as 'idealistic'. He insists that it is impossible to be a good butler and be critical of one's employer, but he is also critical and contemptuous of 'mindless' loyalty. He values 'intelligent loyalty' and distances himself from the fact that Lord Darlington was 'misguided' and also from feeling 'regret' or 'shame' over his employer's mistakes.

> As Stevens opens the **narrative** with a declaration about Lord Darlington's anti-Semitism, of being 'able to refute it with absolute authority', he immediately sets himself up for a contradiction which further adds to his unreliability as a **narrator** (see Narrative Techniques). He strives to play down the seriousness of Lord Darlington's actions using words such as 'absurd allegations' and 'brief, entirely insignificant' (p. 153) with regard to the dismissal of the two Jewish maids. It is **ironic** that when he proceeds to try to demonstrate how 'insignificant' the events are, he actually does the opposite. It is one of the key themes in the novel that apparent trivialities reveal things of greater significance (see Critical

Approaches on Themes). Here is no exception and Stevens cannot or will not see it for himself.

When Lord Darlington tells Stevens to sack the two Jewish employees, Stevens accepts it without protest. Lord Darlington even tries to provide some reasons for his decision, which are thoroughly unsatisfactory, but Stevens still has no objections. This is in stark contrast to the reaction of Miss Kenton, who shows her feelings and protests to Stevens. She calls the proposed action a 'sin' (see Imagery & Symbolism) and implicitly questions Lord Darlington's judgement, to Stevens's consternation. He tells her to remember her place and shows his blind faith in Lord Darlington. He tries to encourage the same in Miss Kenton, but she reveals her independent mind.

Stevens puts all personal feelings – morality, even – to one side for his duty to Lord Darlington. He recounts the actual dismissal of the two maids in a few lines. He reveals no emotion about it and seems to have no heart, as though he is inhuman. Perhaps he feels guilt over it deep down and has repressed these feelings. Miss Kenton punishes him for two weeks for his lack of response and yet her threats to leave come to nothing. Stevens teases her about this as time goes by and perhaps she takes this as a sign that he does not want her to go. She will often 'go quiet', a habit which Stevens interprets as 'embarrassment'; her quietness appears again in the summerhouse where Kazuo Ishiguro uses the **pathetic fallacy** of the fog and the darkness to underpin the theme of blindness. Stevens and Miss Kenton do not see each other or communicate fully. Miss Kenton tries: she opens up to him, reveals something of herself, her cowardice in not leaving, and Stevens does not reciprocate. She mentions 'feeling my whole life is wasting away' (p. 161) but neither of them see that Stevens's own life is wasting away. This is the reality he comes to face by the end of the novel; he knows it deep down, but cannot face it. Miss Kenton reveals that she was afraid to leave for fear of 'finding nobody who knew or cared about me' (p. 161), from which it can be inferred that she feels known and cared about at Darlington Hall – by Stevens, it would seem. She is infuriated when he tells her that Lord Darlington's change of heart is a result of a 'misunderstanding' and how upset he himself was at the time. This was certainly not clear to Miss Kenton or the reader. Her demand for him to share his feelings with her is a plea for him to stop pretending, to be real and honest with her, to lower his barriers and take off his persona of the modest, dutiful and perfect butler and be human. Stevens refuses to allow this and insists on their relationship remaining professional, picking up the tray in the summerhouse and hiding behind his job once more.

We learn a great deal about Miss Kenton in this chapter, from her 'quietness' and frustration with Stevens to her keenness for Lisa to succeed. She seems to be trying to live vicariously through Lisa and is crestfallen when Lisa runs off with the second footman in a romantic gesture of love coupled with noble ideals. Her triumph over Lisa's improvement is short-lived and she appears to have a two-fold response to Lisa's departure. She says Lisa had great potential and that she will only be 'let down'. She seemed to be trying to mould Lisa in her own image. Yet her weary voice betrays perhaps something more. She too is capable of putting up a front: it is difficult for her to admit she is wrong to the 'perfect' Stevens and she seems to be trying to save face and hide the fact that she herself has been let down by Stevens on a personal level. She looks at her hands, as Stevens's father does when he is ill. As in Stevens's father's case, Miss Kenton's hands are a **symbol** of her life's work and they are empty. She has no ring on her finger, no family, no children, nothing to show for her life, but to Stevens she simply seems remote, as he does not see beneath her mask. She is perceptive and sees Stevens's aversion to 'pretty girls', which he dismisses, pointing out that he had 'largely forgotten' Lisa a few months after her arrival; but Miss Kenton wants to discover that he is human, made of 'flesh and blood', instead of being cold and inhuman (pp. 164–5). She pushes him to reveal a warmer, more human side of himself, but he says 'I shall simply place my thoughts elsewhere', his device for avoiding anything he does not wish to face, including his own feelings, which he represses behind his persona.

In the fiercely patriarchal society of 1930s England, a woman had to choose between work and marriage and could not choose both. Her 'job' after marriage was to look after her husband, her children and the home. We learn more about Miss Kenton later in the chapter when Stevens remembers how she tried to bring flowers into his pantry (see also Imagery & Symbolism), which she calls a 'prison cell' (p. 174), the very phrase Stevens uses to describe his father's room on p. 67. Stevens's room, and later his reading material, reflect Stevens's inner self. He has become like his father to an excessive degree. The flowers **symbolise** Miss Kenton's vibrancy, her spirit and her warmth (see Imagery & Symbolism). Her liveliness and Stevens's austerity complement one another, as the flowers in the 'cell' brighten it. Stevens echoes his description of preparing for the 1923 international conference as 'a general might prepare for a battle' (p. 81) when he compares his office to 'a general's headquarters during a battle' (p. 173). He follows it up with military verbs to describe Miss Kenton's 'advance' towards him and her 'marching' into his room. This suggests that other people, and the threat of the emotions they bring with them, are the enemy and need to be resisted. When Miss Kenton barges into his room, she is nosy and insistent, causing him to feel threatened and fearful. She 'invades' his bodily space in order to prise the book from his fingers. The change in the atmosphere which he struggles to articulate is a realisation of intimacy and desire. He cannot cope with it and looks away, both **literally** and **metaphorically**. He insists to the reader that the romantic novel served the purpose of improving his vocabulary, something which he sees as part of his duty. However, he is not entirely convincing as his choice of reading material is very telling. He is reading about love and relationships, things that he has denied himself and perhaps cannot understand. Here, he reveals unwittingly his hidden longing for love and closeness. He even confesses to the pleasure he gains from these 'absurd' stories, which shows his tender side and the need for the warmth and affection he will not allow himself. He does not see this himself and the reader has a growing awareness of a three-fold **narrative** perspective: that of Stevens, who cannot or will not see reality; the reader's own perspective of interpreting and seeing that which Stevens cannot; and the viewpoint of Ishiguro, the author who has deliberately designed the novel in this way. See Narrative Techniques for further discussion.

Stevens continues to consider the change in their relationship and feels that Miss Kenton's days off were a contributing factor. His conversation with Mr Graham reveals his anxiety, although he disguises it with professional concern, and Mr Graham sees what Stevens cannot, that Miss Kenton craves marriage and a family. Stevens dismisses his theory, but is shaken by the notion of a suitor. He cites other clues as proof, such as the letters and her mood swings, but has no real idea of what she is thinking or feeling and does not seem to try. He is unable to **empathise** and yet at other times, such as the fork incident with Mr Farraday and the failed attempt to banter with the locals at the Coach and Horses inn, he agonises over minutiae, sometimes for hours. As yet, the reader is still unaware of the extent and depth of the feelings they have for one another, but with hindsight it is possible to interpret Miss Kenton's behaviour as her being happy to have love-letters and a suitor, in a faint echo of the romantic elopement of Lisa and the footman. However, she wishes Stevens were her suitor and is hoping to provoke a reaction in him with this romance: she is depressed when he does not react. Hence her relief when he asks her about it, in the guise of professional interest, and her revelation that she is dating an ex-butler, whom she has mentally compared to Stevens and found wanting. Stevens seems unaware of the extent of the compliment and its implicit meaning, that she likes Stevens and wishes he were her suitor. Her **ironic**, possibly sarcastic, words to Stevens – that he must be a 'well-contented man' and that she 'really cannot imagine what more you might wish for in life' (p. 182) – are her way of saying that surely he is in need of a wife and this is the one area lacking in his life. She is also implicitly offering herself in that speech, yet Stevens does not take the bait. She has provided him with numerous opportunities to declare himself to her, but his answer is a sombre rejection of her and a re-dedication of himself to Lord Darlington.

Stevens's words 'vocation', 'lordship' and 'the day his lordship's work is complete' reveal the extent of his worship of his employer; he echoes religious fervour here and Lord Darlington seems to have taken on almost Christ-like proportions in his mind (see Imagery & Symbolism). As far as Stevens is concerned, Lord Darlington is not only serving humanity, but he is saving it too. It is no wonder that Miss Kenton's mood changes after this; again, we can see why but Stevens cannot. It is unsurprising that she is 'tired' of the cocoa evenings; this word is used for her reaction to his rejection of her on p. 183, and again on p. 231 for his response to her rejection of him (see Imagery & Symbolism). It forms a linguistic mirror suggesting that they complement one another. Miss Kenton no longer takes pleasure in the cocoa evenings as they now offer no prospect of a relationship with Stevens. Yet, she is reluctant to end them and it is Stevens who does this. He feels threatened by any sort of intimacy and is determined to return the relationship to how it was before his father died. In a mirror image of their former battle of wills, he tells her to leave him written messages. This causes a change in the Stevens of 1956 as he remembers this. He begins to analyse his behaviour, something he has, as yet, not done in the novel; before now he has merely presented the reader with information.

Stevens is still unable to admit that he was wrong, but he does admit to lacking in foresight in the 1930s. This is a small but significant psychological breakthrough for him. It leads him to reflect upon his treatment of Miss Kenton when her aunt dies. He has every good intention towards her grief over this and praises her in his **narrative** on the way she holds her feelings in when she reads the letter; but actual, real emotions are terrifying for Stevens. He says: 'it was not impossible that Miss Kenton … was actually crying. The thought provoked a strange feeling to rise within me' (p. 186). This is his fear of emotions and provides further clues to his behaviour when his father died. He was terrified of losing control and had to hide behind his work to maintain control of the situation and of himself (see Themes). This is similar to what he does here: he hides behind his job and instead of consoling the distraught

Miss Kenton, criticises her work as he used to when she first started at Darlington Hall, hiding his real feelings of terror and indecision as to how to act, with 'another short laugh' (p. 187). To Miss Kenton, though, his rejection of her is complete. He has previously rejected her on a personal level and now it seems as though he is rejecting her on a professional level, saying her work is below standard. To her, he could not be plainer and her expression of 'trying to puzzle out something' (p. 188) is how she realises she has completely misread his feelings for her, including his teasing about her not leaving the Hall after the dismissal of the two Jewish maids. She thought it was a sign that he did not want her to leave and now sees that she was wrong, as she was wrong about Lisa.

Stevens, the reader suspects, can see with hindsight what their conversations were really about, as he retreats firmly with two paragraphs beginning with 'But' (pp. 188–9), and reproaches himself for indulging in a pointless exercise – although he confirms once more that he has read far too much into Miss Kenton's letter. Again, he unwittingly reveals more than he intended to, as he says: 'There was surely nothing to indicate at the time that such evidently small incidents would render whole dreams forever irredeemable' (pp. 188–9). This develops the theme of trivialities denoting important things and also leads the reader to question what these 'dreams' might be. This is the first mention of any 'dreams' connected to Miss Kenton, and implies the horrific loss he has suffered with her departure. It also mirrors her own words to Stevens later, when waiting at the bus stop and thinking about what life might have been like with Stevens (p. 251). Here he seems to be starting to face up to his life and lost opportunities, and inspires great sympathy and compassion.

Stevens's attitude on his holiday has relaxed enough for him to call the Taylors by their names, which is more personal and human than 'landlady', as before. He is also warm towards their 'humble' home, which includes cobwebs, and although this would seem like natural gratitude for their unmerited hospitality toward him, his unforgiving domestic eye does seem to have softened. He continues to pre-empt criticism and justify himself, over his error in running

out of petrol, and when he describes his search for help, Kazuo
Ishiguro includes a poignant description of Stevens's discomfort
at seeing the cosy village with its lights from the 'lonely hill' as
the daylight fades and the mist closes in. These are **metaphors** that
link to the title and the end of the novel. For Stevens, 'the remains
of the day' are his impending old age; the mist is a **symbol** of his
blindness: his inability, his reluctance to face reality. He will
metaphorically remain on a 'lonely hill' apart from the warmth of
humanity if he does not face reality, lower his barriers and reach out
to others.

Stevens's encounter with the villagers begins badly as Mr Taylor
immediately shows his respect for Stevens's apparent status by
touching his cap and referring to Stevens as 'the likes of yourself'
(p. 172). He mistakes Stevens for a gentleman based on his clothes,
just as the other ordinary people Stevens meets en route do, such as
the landlady in Salisbury, and the chauffeur near Mortimer's Pond
who guesses Stevens's real status from the way he talks (p. 125).
Ishiguro interweaves the theme of clothes and appearances into
Stevens's perception of his duty when Stevens states that 'A
butler of any quality must be seen to *inhabit* his role, utterly and
fully' and cannot put it on and cast it off like 'a pantomime
costume' (p. 178). Stevens believes that you become the person
whose clothes you have put on and he demonstrates this when
he allows the Taylors and their neighbours to believe that he really
is a gentleman. It is as though his goal of becoming the perfect
butler, like his father, was modified, when he went to work for
Lord Darlington, into becoming the perfect man. He has
transposed his feelings of worship for his remote, unfeeling father
onto the equally remote Lord Darlington, and until now was
willing to be the perfect butler in the service of the perfect man (see
Imagery & Symbolism). His symbiotic relationship with Lord
Darlington goes a step further here, though, as Stevens pretends to
be him. He demonstrates this with his talk of mixing with men of
influence, such as Winston Churchill and Anthony Eden. This
provides a glimpse of the vanity and egotism lurking behind his
modest façade. Stevens is not above deception to suit his own ends,

as we have seen with Mr Farraday and the Wakefields, but here Stevens is a fraud. He later describes his deception as a 'misunderstanding', the same term used for Lord Darlington's dismissal of the Jewish maids.

The company debates the issue of what makes a true gentleman, an echo of Stevens's preoccupation with 'what is a "great" butler?', and their beliefs include not only appearance but morals and values. **Ironically,** Harry Smith says that the disgraced Mr Lindsay took them 'for fools' (p. 193), but they do not realise how they are being fooled by Stevens. Stevens offers 'dignity' as his definition of a true gentleman, which he earlier offered to the reader as a definition of a great butler. In his mind the two appear as one and the same. There is further irony with Harry Smith's pronouncements on being 'born free' and his comment that 'You can't have dignity if you're a slave' since slaves are not free but are part of the oppressive class system. Stevens, who prides himself on his dignity, enslaved himself in his service and devotion to Lord Darlington, taking his duty to his employer to an excessive degree. All of this and the references to Hitler serve as reminders of Lord Darlington and the danger he exposed England to. **Ironically,** he could have done so much good, could have served humanity, but was foolish and weak. Harry Smith unwittingly underlines the gravity of Lord Darlington's folly when he says: 'For the likes of yourself, it's always been easy to exert your influence. You can count the most powerful in the land as your friends' (p. 199).

Harry Smith's views are fiercely democratic and are in direct contrast to Lord Darlington's fascist opinions which are expressed in this same chapter. Stevens veers towards those of Lord Darlington and even suggests that the reader should do the same: 'you and I will never be in a position to comprehend the great affairs of today's world, and our best course will always be to put our trust in an employer we judge to be wise and honourable' (p. 211). The 'you' remains an intriguing puzzle (see Narrative Techniques), but it seems certain from these words that Stevens is addressing a fellow servant. Stevens escapes the scrutinising gaze of Dr Carlisle and feels great 'discomfort' over it – deservedly so, the reader might think. He recalls an incident when he is mocked by Mr Spencer in front of Lord Darlington and this relates back to his words in Salisbury when he describes how some butlers have been 'displayed as a kind of performing monkey at a house party' (p. 36). His words then bore the distinct implication that he was spared this treatment, that Lord Darlington never treated him in such a way. Clearly, the reader has to be careful not to take Stevens's words at face value, as any such implication has been firmly contradicted here. Mr Spencer's behaviour is a spiteful and an unnecessary 'demonstration' of the supposed folly of democracy, that the ordinary person could and should have no say in politics, and it is sanctioned by Lord Darlington, who summoned Stevens for this display and silently witnesses it. He does, however, apologise to Stevens the next day, in a direct parallel to the apology made by the drunken gentlemen to Stevens's father. Stevens declares to the reader that the humiliation at the hands of Mr Spencer was merely a 'slightly uncomfortable situation' (p. 206), which is reminiscent of his previous understatements, but the reader by now is not taken in by it. This is his 'persona' talking, his modest, dutiful, devoted persona. Hidden underneath is the anger and pain that constitute his real feelings. Lord Darlington's apology is couched in an explanation that is intended to appease and compliment the dutiful Stevens, that he 'did assist in demonstrating a very important point ... if the likes of Sir Leonard are made to wake up and think a little, then you can take it from me your ordeal last night was not in vain' (p. 207). The irony of Stevens again helping in his employer's downfall is clear: Stevens has apparently 'helped' to convince the pro-democratic Sir Leonard to adopt fascist views, which Lord Darlington goes on to explain and endorse. This shows the reader conclusively that he was not the gullible gentleman who was influenced by the likes of Carolyn Barnet and who realised the true 'ugly' nature of fascism, as Stevens would have us believe. It may well have begun that way, but Lord Darlington was a true fascist at heart, as Stevens's words in this chapter confirm. Stevens tacitly acknowledges this by saying that in 1956 they are 'unattractive' ideas, before hiding behind his duty again.

In one long paragraph over three pages (209–11), which is a sign of
the depth of his feelings that come pouring out here, Stevens reveals
cowardice and self-loathing by insisting that it was not his place
to question or criticise his employer but merely to do his job well.
He insists that he had to put his own judgements aside for the sake
of his career, but he contradicts himself here by condemning
'mindless' loyalty and implying that he found an employer who
'embodies all that I find noble and admirable' (pp. 210–11). His
views are very confused. Clearly, he did believe Lord Darlington
was the noble person he appeared to be. Stevens did follow him
with mindless loyalty. If he had not, he could have left his post and
transferred to another, more agreeable, one. He did put his feelings
aside, not for his career, but in order to be a perfect butler and one
worthy of Lord Darlington, whom he looked up to. Stevens did
trust him to be 'wise' and 'honourable', but is implying that he
knows Lord Darlington was not. Yet he is still loath to actually state
this boldly. He goes as far as saying that Lord Darlington was
'misguided' and 'foolish' and admits that his life and work appear 'a
sad waste', but he absolves himself of blame and refuses to see that
he too was wrong and his own life is equally 'a sad waste'. He gave
himself totally to what he thought was good, but actually it was
not; the sacrifice was not worth it. This is the reality that Stevens
must try to face and accept. He distances himself completely from
Lord Darlington, denying any close association with him, and this
denial to the reader is the third in the novel. The analogy to Peter
in the New Testament Book of Mark, with three denials of
Lord Darlington, is complete (see Imagery & Symbolism), and
particularly **ironic**, considering everything he has claimed earlier in
the novel. Stevens is lifting off his mask and a muddled mess of
repressed feelings has come tumbling out. His rejection of Lord
Darlington seems to be beyond that of Peter, however, and more
like that of Pontius Pilate, who washed his hands of Jesus and let
the people do as they wished.

Mr Churchill Sir Winston Leonard Spencer Churchill (1874–1965) first
entered Parliament as a Conservative MP in 1900, before joining the Liberal
Party in 1904. He served as Colonial Under-Secretary, President of the

Board of Trade and Home Secretary before becoming the First Lord of the Admiralty in 1911. After the First World War, during which he authorised the disastrous Gallipoli campaign, he was Secretary of State for War and Air, and Chancellor of the Exchequer, before rejoining the Conservatives in 1929. He succeeded Neville Chamberlain as Prime Minister on 10 May 1940 and led Britain through the Second World War until losing office in the 1945 election. He later served again as Prime Minister, from 1951 until 1955, when he returned to the back benches

Mr Eden Sir Robert Anthony Eden (1897–1977) became parliamentary under-secretary of the Foreign Office in 1931, Lord Privy Seal and Privy Councillor in 1934, and Secretary of State for foreign affairs in 1935. He resigned from this position in 1938 after disagreeing with Prime Minister Neville Chamberlain over the signing of the Munich Agreement. He was appointed Secretary of State for War in 1940 and was Minister of Foreign Affairs from 1940 to 1945 and leader of the House of Commons from 1942 to 1945. In 1955 he succeeded Winston Churchill as Prime Minister and the following year, when Stevens's **narrative** is written, ordered British forces to occupy the Suez Canal Zone, in collaboration with France and Israel, an action condemned by the United Nations (see Historical Background)

the Empire from the sixteenth to the twentieth centuries, Britain ruled over many countries, colonies, dominions and territories collectively known as the British Empire. It fell into decline after the First World War as countries demanded and received independence from it. In 1931 the dominions achieved effective independence, and Parliament reorganised the Empire into the Commonwealth of Nations, which still exists today. The Asian colonies gained independence shortly after the Second World War, and most of the rest of the British Empire was decolonised in the 1960s

M. Laval Pierre Laval (1883–1945). A politician who was initially on the extreme left of the French Socialist Party, he gradually moved to the right of the political spectrum, and served as Prime Minister of France in 1931–2 and 1935–6. In 1940 he became Pétain's deputy in the Vichy government. As Prime Minister again, from 1942 to 1944, Laval collaborated with the Nazi regime, and at the end of the Second World War fled to Germany and Spain, before being recaptured and executed in Paris on a charge of treason

President Roosevelt Franklin Delano Roosevelt (1882–1945) was the thirty-second President of the United States, from 1933 to 1945. He was re-elected three times and rescued America from the Economic Depression of the 1930s with the 'New Deal'. In 1940, he involved America in the Second World War through his legislation of lend-lease, providing economic aid to the Allies, but it was the Japanese attack on Pearl Harbor on 7 December 1941 that provoked America's military involvement in the war

Day four – afternoon (little compton, cornwall)

> At the Rose Garden Hotel, Stevens reveals that Dr Carlisle recognised that he was not a genuine gentleman, but chose not to betray him and even helped him to progress on his journey. Stevens recalls a visit from Mr Cardinal and Herr Ribbentrop to Darlington Hall, on the same evening that Miss Kenton decided to marry Mr Benn

The narrative resumes with Stevens stating that he is in Little Compton, in the Rose Garden Hotel. He is anticipating his meeting with Miss Kenton and pauses to describe how Dr Carlisle picked him up in his Rover to fetch petrol for Mr Farraday's Ford.

While this takes place, Dr Carlisle reveals that he had, in fact, seen through Stevens's 'act' the night before but chose not to let on. It is established that Stevens is the butler at Darlington Hall and they discuss Harry Smith's political views and the concept of dignity. Dr Carlisle admits to having socialist views, but they have been tempered over time. Stevens gives his own view of dignity, they get the petrol and Stevens follows Dr Carlisle in the Ford in order to pick up the right road, entering Cornwall at about nine o'clock in the morning.

Stevens is overwhelmed by his memories of Miss Kenton, now that he is so close to seeing her again. He realises that a previously mentioned memory, that of his hesitation outside Miss Kenton's door as she is crying, has not been accurately recounted after all, and he proceeds to describe the incident as it happened more accurately. It occurred at a similar time in 1936, but on a different evening, one where Reginald Cardinal, whose father had been killed in a riding accident around 1932, arrived unexpectedly at the Hall.

Miss Kenton tells Stevens that her acquaintance has asked her to marry him and becomes angry when Stevens gives little response to this news. Stevens resumes his post at Lord Darlington's side, noting that there is an unusual tension between his employer and Mr Cardinal. Some very distinguished guests arrive, including Herr Ribbentrop. Later, Miss Kenton returns with the news that she has accepted her suitor's proposal of marriage and when Stevens again gives no response, she cruelly tells him what a figure of fun he is to her and her fiancé. Meanwhile Mr Cardinal requires more brandy and drunkenly tells Stevens that it is the Prime Minister and the Foreign Secretary who are secretly meeting Herr Ribbentrop and that Lord Darlington is 'being made a fool of'. He has been trying to persuade the Prime Minister to visit Hitler and the secret talks are about a proposed visit by the King to see Hitler. Stevens insists it is not his position to think, question or even notice the Nazis and that he trusts Lord Darlington's judgement on such matters.

When Stevens goes towards the cellar to fetch some port, Miss Kenton emerges and apologises for her cruel words. Stevens hurries on, but as he retraces his steps with the port, he hesitates outside her door, convinced she is crying. He then proceeds onwards with the port and attends to the gentleman thereafter, feeling low in spirits at first, and then triumphant at his own dignity that evening. He feels proud to be assisting Lord Darlington, who is at the 'hub' of power, and feels himself to be at the pinnacle of his career.

> Stevens's **narrative** voice has resumed a formal tone with vocabulary such as 'partake of', 'commenced lunch', 'ascertained' and 'residing' (pp. 215–16). He is very precise about his whereabouts, time (it is 2.20pm) and situation. His persona has returned, as he is anxious about seeing Miss Kenton again; perhaps he is also retreating behind it because he has revealed so much of himself at the end of the last chapter. He agonises over the impending meeting, but changes the subject to safer topics, such as the weather, before recapping the morning's events. Similarly, he skips over the details of his journey into Cornwall, because he is obsessed and preoccupied by Miss Kenton.

Dr Carlisle provides an interesting contrast to Lord Darlington's friend, Mr Spencer, in the previous chapter. He is a gentleman and a professional, but acts decently. He calls Stevens 'old boy' and 'old fellow', familiar terms used between equals, even after revealing he knows Stevens is a butler. The previous night, in front of his neighbours, the locals, and on 'home territory', he had a prime opportunity to ridicule and humiliate Stevens, as Mr Spencer did, but he did not take it. He guessed the truth, but went along with Stevens's show, even standing up with the others out of respect when Stevens left the room to go to bed. Dr Carlisle displays truly gentlemanly behaviour, unlike Lord Darlington and those he surrounds himself with. Dr Carlisle is also in touch with the times politically, having relaxed his socialist views, although he seems disappointed in the underlying political apathy of the local people, despite the strong talk. Ultimately, he appears to be decent, gentlemanly and warm, a true humanist.

Stevens's response to the question from Dr Carlisle about dignity centres on clothing, that dignity involves 'not removing one's clothing in public' (p. 221). This **metaphor** could be Stevens attempting banter with the jolly, bemused Dr Carlisle, particularly as it is Stevens's clothes, as well as his behaviour, that led to the misunderstanding earlier (see Imagery & Symbolism). The **irony** is, though, that Stevens metaphorically never removes his butler's garb, even when alone (see also Themes). This was demonstrated when Miss Kenton entered his pantry and when he stayed in the guest house in Salisbury.

Stevens goes back to the memory of his hesitation outside Miss Kenton's room, which has been bothering him. He has openly contradicted himself and is at pains to correct himself (see Narrative Techniques). Once again, the personal and the professional collide on a fateful evening that echoes the international conference of 1923 when his father died. The appearance of Reginald Cardinal reminds the reader of the humorous encounters he and Stevens had during that conference, but this time, events are more serious, sombre and tragic. This is a turning point in Stevens's life, as he loses Miss Kenton, while Mr Cardinal reveals to Stevens the true and dangerous extent of Lord Darlington's affiliation with the Nazis, which will cause his downfall.

Miss Kenton tells Stevens of Mr Benn's proposal and is crushed when there is no reaction from Stevens. She is thus pushed into accepting Mr Benn, as there is **literally** and **metaphorically** 'nothing before her' (p. 224) if she stays with Stevens. Her hands will remain 'empty' (see Imagery & Symbolism). She is weighing up her options and her future and provides Stevens with the opportunity to help her make up her mind, which he does, but not as she intends. Thus her question to him about remaining in the Hall that evening is a loaded one. She is asking him whether she should refuse Mr Benn or not and Stevens, by telling her there is no reason for her not to go, implicitly tells her to accept the offer of marriage. His attention is focused, typically, on Lord Darlington, Mr Cardinal and the distinguished visitors who arrive that evening. He does not seem to realise that he poses Miss Kenton an equally loaded question when she returns, impeded by the policeman helping to provide security for the Prime Minister and Foreign Secretary. She is keen to tell Stevens that she has accepted Mr Benn but he puts duty first. He hides behind his work with his persona firmly in place, giving no reaction, except one of calm politeness and concern for his duty. He makes it absolutely clear to her that Lord Darlington is more important than she is and thus she can see the true waste in waiting for him all these years. She has made the right decision, but it is also the wrong decision, as she loves Stevens, and deep down, below the persona, Stevens loves her, although as yet the reader is not fully aware of this. She can have no future with Stevens, but in accepting Mr Benn she is giving up the love of her life and marrying a man she does not love. Her cruel words to Stevens are those of a woman scorned and show the depth of her pain. Stevens reveals the depth of his loss of her and his reaction to her cruel words when he tells Mr Cardinal he is 'tired', the same word that Miss Kenton uses on p. 183 when Stevens has rejected her (see Imagery & Symbolism). This exhaustion is a sign of emotional upheaval. Mr Cardinal notices Stevens's distress, as he and Lord Darlington did after Stevens's father died during the 1923 international conference. The parallel between these events is marked.

Stevens is shown the true waste in serving Lord Darlington with such devotion and self-sacrifice all these years, when Mr Cardinal tells him of Lord Darlington's folly. In trying to persuade the Prime Minister and the King to strengthen ties with Hitler, Lord Darlington is playing a dangerous game with the fate of the country, and Mr Lewis's prophetic words of 1923 have come true, as Mr Cardinal admits. We are reminded that Lord Darlington's motives are pure, but his actions are dangerous. Stevens doggedly refuses to see Mr Cardinal's point of view, demonstrating the 'mindless sort of "loyalty"' (p. 210) he is contemptuous of in Moscombe. This could also be interpreted as a denial of reality, that he simply cannot face the truth. The reader, though, has a new perception of Lord Darlington and Stevens's defence of him in the light of this information needs to be re-evaluated.

Stevens, typically, misinterprets Miss Kenton's insomnia as he fetches the port. He does not or will not realise that his conduct over the marriage proposal, rather than his footsteps, is what is keeping her awake. He rebuffs her apology by insisting he cannot recall her words and puts her in her place again, below Lord Darlington. His assistance with the matters of 'great importance', however, merely amounts to fetching port, just as he proffered port in 1923 as his father died. His presence and the port he is in charge of are trivialities which he focuses on while losing his father and Miss Kenton forever (see Themes). He appears completely heartless and inhuman as he hesitates outside her room, but it is the presence of her dangerous emotions that have caused him to repress his real feelings and hide behind his butler's persona. This is his second 'tiger under the table' incident, whereby he feels he demonstrates true dignity and the fact that he is at the top of his career, causing him to feel as triumphant as he did after the 1923 international conference. However, this triumph seems even emptier than that of 1923: he has lost Miss Kenton and he refuses to see that he is wasting his life serving Lord Darlington.

Prime Minister Stanley Baldwin, First Earl Baldwin of Bewdley
(1867–1947). He was Prime Minister from 1923 to 1924, 1924 to 1929,
and 1935 to 1937 and was against the proposed marriage of King Edward
VIII to Wallis Simpson. He was instrumental in bringing about the
abdication of the King and was criticised for ignoring Germany's
re-armament

Foreign Secretary Anthony Eden (see 'Mr Eden' on p. 50 of this Note)

our new king Edward VIII (1894–1972), the eldest son of George V. He was
king from 20 January 1936 until 11 December 1936. He abdicated so that
he could marry the twice-divorced American Wallis Simpson (the wedding
took place in France in June 1937), and he became known as the Duke of
Windsor. As Reginald Cardinal states, Edward was known for his Nazi
sympathies; in 1937, after his abdication, he visited Adolf Hitler and
inspected social conditions in Germany. He was appointed Governor of the
Bahamas during the Second World War, following which he became friends
with Sir Oswald Mosley, who had established the British Union of Fascists
in 1932 (see also Historical Background)

the Rhineland in 1936 Germany remilitarised the Rhineland, an area
around the river Rhine in Germany, breaking the Treaty of Versailles

Day six – evening (weymouth)

Stevens is sitting on the pier, and describes his meeting
with Miss Kenton two days ago. A retired butler strikes up
a conversation with Stevens, and Stevens admits that he
gave everything to Lord Darlington. The former butler
encourages him to enjoy the remains of his day and when
the pier lights come on, Stevens decides to face the future
and learn to banter

Stevens begins this final chapter with the information that he is on the
pier at Weymouth and has been walking around on it for half an hour,
but as the lights will shortly be switched on, he is now sitting on a bench
with a good view of the sea and the evening sky. He goes on to say that
he arrived in Weymouth the previous day and has decided to stay for an
extra day to enjoy a break from driving. He plans to return to Darlington
Hall the next morning. Stevens tells us how he met Miss Kenton at the
Rose Garden Hotel in Little Compton two days ago.

Miss Kenton comes to the hotel and they talk in the tea lounge for two hours. She, of course, looks older, but also seems calmer and less fiery, with a noticeable sadness in her eyes and face. As they talk, Stevens learns that her marriage is not coming to an end. She did leave her husband for some days but went back to him. He is due to take early retirement through ill health and her daughter, Catherine, who lives in Dorset, is married and pregnant and would love to meet Stevens. Stevens tells Miss Kenton about the changes at Darlington Hall. He tells her that Mr Cardinal was killed in Belgium during the Second World War and mentions the decline of Lord Darlington. During the war he bore the criticisms of a newspaper for his Nazism and sued it once the war was over, losing the libel action against the newspaper. This ruined his name and he became almost an invalid.

After two hours, Stevens drives Miss Kenton to her bus stop and on the way he expresses the fact that he had been worried about her, due to her letter; Miss Kenton reassures him that she is happy and fulfilled, with a grandchild to look forward to. Stevens says he has only work to look forward to and as they wait for the bus, he asks her how her husband treats her, because she has left her husband several times. She again reassures him and realises he is asking her whether or not she loves her husband. She says that although she did not at first, she has 'grown to love him'. She admits to sometimes feeling that she has made a mistake and that she could have had a better life, a life with Stevens. Stevens's heart breaks at these words, but he hides it and tells her they cannot go back, that he does not want to come between her and her husband. He tells her that they must both (Stevens and Miss Kenton) value what they have, and that she has so much in her life with much to look forward to. In tears, Miss Kenton leaves by bus.

On the pier in Weymouth, Stevens has fallen into conversation with a man who voices the opinion that the evening is the best time of the day. The man explains he was a butler of a modest house in Weymouth until three years before, and Stevens reveals his own status. A discussion about being a butler ensues and Stevens admits that he gave Lord Darlington the best he had and has very little left to give. The errors occurring under Mr Farraday's employ are the signs to Stevens that he has given everything, his whole life, to Lord Darlington. Stevens cries and the butler is sympathetic. Stevens pours out his feelings to him, admitting that he blindly followed Lord Darlington and that he has no real dignity. The butler tells him to look forward, into the evening, to enjoy the remains of his day.

Twenty minutes after the butler's departure, Stevens is still sitting on the pier, the lights have come on and he reflects upon what the man has said. Stevens accepts that he cannot change the past, and feels that at least he tried to do something worthwhile with his life. He notices the people enjoying themselves around him and sees that they are strangers who strike up conversations using banter. He sees its value, as it is 'the key to human warmth', and feels enthusiastic about trying it again, deciding to put his heart into it. The novel closes with Stevens's vow to practise it again when he returns to Darlington Hall the next day, so that he can surprise Mr Farraday when he returns from America in a week's time.

> Miss Kenton and Stevens retain their usual politeness towards one another during their reunion, although Miss Kenton has lost her fiery spirit and seems subdued. Stevens relearns her ways and he also discovers that her marriage is not over, as he thinks and hopes, despite the fact that she did leave her husband for some days before returning to him. The fact that he refers to her in his **narrative** as Miss Kenton, despite using her married name (Mrs Benn) when speaking to her, suggests that he cannot properly accept the reality of her present circumstances. Stevens tries to remind us that he has professional reasons for seeing her again and they exchange news. Reginald Cardinal's death in the Second World War and Lord Darlington's unsuccessful libel action, his fall from grace, become mere asides now, and Miss Kenton takes her rightful place as a main character in the **narrative**, for we learn of the true feelings that they have for one another. Although Miss Kenton has much to look forward to, with a grandchild on the way and her husband taking early retirement (although due to ill health), she reveals that she often feels her life has been a mistake and she wonders about a life with Stevens. Stevens's heart breaks on hearing this. Considering the incredible politeness they always maintain, these are, for them, declarations of love that alter the reader's perceptions and colour all the conversations they have

exchanged until now (see Narrative Techniques). Kazuo Ishiguro handles this exchange with tender **pathos**, heightened by their restraint and politeness. **Ironically**, Miss Kenton always returns to her husband out of duty, just as Stevens sacrificed her out of duty. She loves Mr Benn, but is not truly in love with him. She is in love with Stevens, who loves her in return. Stevens covers his heartbreak with a typical smile to hide his pain. At last he feels real emotion, which he shows to the reader, but not to Miss Kenton – she never knows how he feels for her. He is confronted by the fact that he sacrificed her for Lord Darlington, who was not worth it. His pain and grief are such that he cannot look at her, except for a glance, which reveals her own pain and grief through her tears, as the bus stops. Miss Kenton's daughter's reported eagerness to meet Stevens may be a sign that Miss Kenton has confided her true feelings for him to her daughter, perhaps in an attempt to explain her behaviour. Stevens again projects his own hidden feelings of 'emptiness' onto her when he quotes from her letter as they are driving to the bus stop.

When Stevens says that he has only work to look forward to, he seems almost to have become his father, who was still working at the age of seventy-two in 1923. The appearance of the retired butler at the end is a clear indication of how society has changed: the possibility of retirement is now a reality in 1956, although Stevens's despair at having nothing left to give to Mr Farraday shows how he feels he is nothing if he cannot work and work well, like his father after his fall. The retired butler, like Mr Benn, who is an ex-butler also, provides an example of an alternative butler's lifestyle – to Stevens and to the reader – of how Stevens's life might have been. He is his alter ego, who did not sacrifice himself for his work and his employer. He is enjoying his retirement and has a positive, satisfied outlook on life, which Stevens could have had if he had not been so obsessive about his father and Lord Darlington. He believes it is not too late for Stevens, though, and urges him to change his frame of mind. The butler has not heard of Lord Darlington and thus there is no need for Stevens to feel defensive and deny working for him. Furthermore, the man did not realise that Stevens was a butler and perhaps even thought he was a gentleman, but he nevertheless opened up a conversation using banter, feeling no inferiority of status. He 'saves' Stevens from a 'fall' (see Imagery & Symbolism) into despair and possibly suicide, as Stevens sits on the pier facing reality and staring into the abyss-like waste that is his life, with nothing to look forward to. Stevens at last shows his feelings to the reader, to the ex-butler and to the world when he cries, removing his persona to talk honestly and frankly to one of his peers. We can compare this encounter with a nameless man with the unsuccessful one on pp. 25–6, as a yardstick for measuring how far Stevens has come on this **literal** and **metaphorical** journey (see Imagery & Symbolism). The differences are clear, in terms of language, attitude, persona and real feelings; perhaps talking to a fellow butler helps Stevens at the end, but the change in him cannot be denied.

During this chapter, Stevens is sitting on the pier at Weymouth in the evening looking out to sea, which links to the **metaphor** of the novel's title. The sea is a **symbol** of life and it is no coincidence that Stevens has left the safety of the shore at this time now that he is facing the truth and reality. He is 'out on a limb'. The evening is a metaphor for old age, as the man suggests, and Ishiguro provides a further **image** in this chapter, that of the lights being switched on. The conversation with the man who 'saves' Stevens and tells him to enjoy his old age leads to Stevens pondering and inwardly digesting his words just as the lights are switched on, as though the 'light has dawned' on Stevens. Prompted by the man's words, he talks himself back from the brink of despair, coming to accept the past and gain a more philosophical attitude about it. He again refers to 'you and I' twice at this time, as though he is talking to one of his peers, perhaps to the retired butler who accepted and comforted him, or to Miss Kenton, in an echo of his words to her at the bus stop, where he urged her to make her sacrifice count for something (see Narrative Techniques).

The final **image** in the chapter is that of banter, the unifying theme that has permeated the novel, culminating here with Stevens 'seeing' it for its true worth as the 'key to human warmth' (see

Themes). He seems to realise that the way to have happiness in life is by lowering one's barriers, reaching out to fellow human beings and communicating with them, using banter as a starting point. This is how the retired butler began a conversation with Stevens. Ishiguro plays upon the word 'fall' by saying that the people on the pier 'proceeded to fall into conversation' (p. 257), and having pulled back from falling into despair, Stevens will, from now on, instead fall into conversation. He plans to improve his bantering skills with 'commitment' and he will put his heart into it. The novel ends on an ambiguous note, however. On the one hand it can be seen as a hopeful ending, as Stevens has examined his life, found it wanting and plans to make changes, using banter. On the other hand, though, it is possible to view the ending as being a sad one, since Stevens's final tragedy is that he intends to use his improved bantering skills on Mr Farraday only and so he is, potentially, about to go full circle. He will end up where he started, doing his duty. He certainly has not taken on board any notions of retiring like the man on the pier, or Mr Benn, and so we are left with the concept of him remaining like his father: we feel that, in spite of banter, he will work until he dies and may even die at work, like his father did, a sombre and tragic end to his 'day'.

PART THREE

CRITICAL APPROACHES

CHARACTERISATION

STEVENS

Stevens is the central character in the novel and also the **narrator** of the plot. He is a complex figure and the reader must 'read between the lines' to see the truth: Stevens, as narrator, consciously selects the material he presents to us, combining a personal 'travel diary' of his driving holiday to Cornwall with memories of the past that reveal more than Stevens intends. He attempts to control everything as principal character and narrator, but in fact betrays himself: the sparseness of his **narrative** (as exemplified by his extreme unwillingness to reveal personal details about himself) is in itself revealing. This 'dual' narrative reveals a significant lack of self-awareness. For example, Stevens seems unaware of how humorous his attempts to explain the facts of life to Reginald Cardinal are, or his practising 'banter' and wit in his room, and he is at a loss to explain an intimate moment with Miss Kenton: 'I am afraid it is not easy to describe clearly what I mean here' (p. 175). Until they meet in Cornwall, he never really knows Miss Kenton and his descriptions of their conversations show how much he misunderstands her and fails to 'see' her, because his own eyes are upon something else: being a perfect butler, like his father, serving – and in fact emulating – Lord Darlington.

Stevens's life is controlled by his own vision of what he ought to be, and being a perfect butler does not include getting married or having children, for example. However, his father – Stevens's first role model – was (probably) married and had two children. Lord Darlington has replaced Stevens's father as a role model and Stevens idolises him. In psychoanalytical terms, it can be said that the coldness of Stevens's relationship with his father, to the point that Stevens addresses him in the third person, has created enormous emotional needs within Stevens and he has created barriers around himself by pursuing to excess a vision and a goal which preclude him from having a family, or from creating an identity away from his work. The personal and professional collide and merge in Stevens's psyche; he has no life, goals or identity apart from being a butler. This causes further barriers and thus he is unable to 'banter'. He cannot speak as himself or even offer opinions, except as a butler – a favourite word is the neutral and ambiguous 'indeed'.

Stevens's chronic isolation and raging emotional needs, as a human being and as the son of a cold and distant father, are channelled into a powerful bond, which transcends hero-worship, focused upon Lord Darlington. It is a symbiotic relationship, whereby they depend on each other: Lord Darlington for unquestioning loyalty and support from his employee, and Stevens for a purpose, role model and identity. However, Stevens wants to be Lord Darlington and even pretends to be a gentleman like him whilst on his journey to Cornwall. One of the **ironies** of the novel and something that Stevens cannot face is that the man he worshipped as a god was, in fact, flawed, a fallible human being after all, and the **narrative** reveals Stevens's refusal to face this. He refuses to admit this because to do so would be to admit that Stevens has completely wasted his life – that he gave up his chance of marriage and children, of true love even, for his life as Lord Darlington's butler, and Lord Darlington proved to be unworthy. This is a truth he cannot bear or face and he has spent most of his life since Lord Darlington's 'fall' denying it.

The car journey takes on the perspective of a psychological or 'inner' journey, which is Kazuo Ishiguro's key **metaphor** (see also Imagery & Symbolism). As Stevens travels to see Miss Kenton, he travels psychologically closer and closer towards this terrible truth. He faces the woman he loved, who loved him in return, whom he gave up, and finally admits to himself what he has known all along. He comes face to face with himself, with the reality that is his life, and sees it for its waste and emptiness.

Miss kenton

Miss Kenton is revealed to the reader through Stevens's memories of the past and through their meeting towards the end of the novel, where we learn that his account of her letter has been inaccurate and largely the result of his wishful thinking. Stevens's memories reveal her to be strong-willed and determined. She stands up to his criticisms of her work quite vehemently. She is also emotional, but without being excessively sentimental. She is in many ways Stevens's diametrical opposite, in that just as he strives to repress and hide his feelings, as part of being a perfect butler, she shows her feelings, and thus has an identity and purpose other than work. She is a thinking, feeling woman capable of anger, irritation and tenderness.

The reader is forced to read between the lines of Stevens's **narrative** to 'see' the real Miss Kenton, whom Stevens constantly misunderstands, and what the reader sees is a woman who has fallen in love with him. She is ready for marriage, and is frequently exasperated by Stevens's wish to keep her at a distance. Again and again she valiantly attempts to grow closer to him, to get to know him, and her efforts become more and more desperate as she senses her youth slipping away and feels the emptiness of her life and the bleakness of her future. She is blind to the fact that Stevens is driven by the desire to be a perfect butler and that he has a symbiotic relationship with Lord Darlington that she can never break. Marriage and children are simply not on the agenda for Stevens because he has psychologically merged the personal and the professional to an excessive degree. Her frustration with Stevens turns to anger and spite when it is apparent that she will never succeed and that she has therefore been wasting her time pursuing him. She is courted by Mr Benn and she hopes this will make Stevens jealous, but even the news of his proposal to her provokes only a 'professional' response from Stevens, to her sorrow and fury. When Stevens meets her in Cornwall, she reveals how she only grew to love Mr Benn after some years of marriage and her telling statement, 'I get to thinking about a life I might have had with you, Mr Stevens' (p. 251), shows the depth of her love and her sorrow for what has been lost. This statement finally provokes an emotional reaction from Stevens as he tells the reader – but not Miss Kenton – 'my heart was breaking'; but she has created a happy life for herself and has a daughter and a grandchild to enjoy in her old age.

Miss Kenton is thus a key figure both for what she reveals about Stevens and in her own right. She, too, is an embodiment of 'dignity', combining this quality and others to be a warm, vibrant, strong woman who is both appealing and admirable.

LORD DARLINGTON

Lord Darlington is the former owner of Darlington Hall, who is deceased at the time Stevens comes to write his narrative. Like Stevens's father, Lord Darlington is revealed to the reader only through Stevens's flashbacks. He is a member of the English aristocracy and seems to embody the terms 'dignity' and 'Englishness', with their cultural connotations of honour, decency, fair play, stiff upper lip and playing the game. He had German friends before the First World War, who suffered dreadfully after the war due to the Treaty of Versailles (see Historical Background). The suffering of friends such as Herr Bremann, who commits suicide, is presented as the motivation for what later becomes Nazi sympathies. Lord Darlington's sense of fair play is violated by the relentless Treaty of Versailles and he feels very strongly that Germany has suffered enough. This leads to the international conference of 1923 where the American, Mr Lewis, calls him an 'amateur'. Sadly, Lewis is right: Lord Darlington is dealing with political matters beyond his limit, because he assumes that other people are adhering to the same codes that he is – codes of decency, fair play and so forth. He has no comprehension of what the Nazi party or Adolf Hitler are really about, such as the 'purification' of the German race, nor the methods they employ. Lord Darlington does not see what is really going on in Germany and, like Stevens, he is blinded by his own vision. In this case, the vision is one of metaphorically shaking hands with Germany in a gesture of 'good sportsmanship' and then getting on as neighbours again, rather than punishing and despising Germany as a defeated enemy. His motives are decent and altruistic, but he is oblivious to the reality of Nazism, and chooses to go along with some of it blindly, to the point of firing two of his maids because they are Jewish.

A modern reader's hindsight allows for alarm and horror at the revelation that Lord Darlington 'has been trying to persuade the Prime Minister ... to accept an invitation to visit Herr Hitler' and that 'his lordship is discussing the idea of His Majesty himself visiting Herr Hitler' (pp. 235–6). He is not as innocent or gullible as Stevens would like the reader to believe, after all. Stevens's blind faith in Lord Darlington is revealed here, although he denies this later on. Lord Darlington's involvement in politics ends inevitably with a 'fall from

grace' by being publicly exposed as a Nazi sympathiser. He is also blind
to Stevens's obsessive devotion to him.

STEVENS'S FATHER

Stevens's father trained Stevens as a footman. He has spent his whole life
in service and, despite a marriage and two sons, has nothing to show for
it. He continues to work at the age of seventy-two and even dies at work.
His room at Darlington Hall is described as a 'prison', the same word that
Miss Kenton uses to describe Stevens's pantry. Stevens is blind to the
realities of his father's life, choosing to focus instead upon his father's
'dignity' in once having chastised three drunken gentlemen who had the
audacity to insult their host, his employer. He also displayed
such dignity when he served the very General who had caused the death
of his son Leonard to such a 'professional' degree that the General
complimented him both verbally and financially. Stevens's father would
fondly retell a story about a butler in India who encountered a tiger under
a table and yet still acted impeccably, and this story is the key to his
professional outlook on life. It is adopted by his son to excess as Stevens
applies this example to both his personal and his professional life, unlike
his father, who (we can assume) did marry. There is no mention of a
Mrs Stevens whatsoever in the novel and she is conspicuous by her
absence.

Stevens's father is quite cold and distant to Stevens, allowing
himself to be addressed in the third person by his son. Although on his
deathbed he tells Stevens 'I'm proud of you. A good son. I hope I've been
a good father to you' (p. 101), Stevens is quite unable to acknowledge
these words, and repeats throughout the brief exchange that he is glad his
father is 'feeling better'. Clearly, Stevens senior has not made a habit of
speaking to his son on a personal level in the past - had he done
so Stevens would be able to respond to the sentiment expressed here.
Yet Stevens is proud and defensive of his father, which is particularly
noticeable in the battle of wills with Miss Kenton. The battle focuses on
the death of Stevens's father – because it coincides with the international
conference, it gives the reader insights into the lengths to which,
professionally, Stevens is prepared to go. Love, marriage and children are
all sacrificed to Stevens's vision, and his father's death is no exception.

Stevens refuses to allow it to distract him from his post as butler at Lord Darlington's side. Miss Kenton is witness to all this, but refuses to see the implications for herself, that if Stevens's own father's death cannot distract him from his purpose, then she too will be unsuccessful.

MINOR CHARACTERS

The minor characters in *The Remains of the Day* can be divided into two categories: those at Darlington Hall in its heyday, such as Lisa, the Jewish servants and Reginald Cardinal; and those people whom Stevens meets on his motoring trip, such as the old man, the Taylors, Dr Carlisle and the retired butler on the pier at Weymouth.

The characters at Darlington Hall provide insights into events and other characters. The Jewish maids, for example, reveal the extent of Lord Darlington's dangerous gullibility as far as Nazism is concerned. Lisa reveals Miss Kenton's 'pride before a fall' as she is so determined to see Lisa succeed, to spite Stevens. She also reveals Miss Kenton's loneliness for love, when she runs off with the second footman. Reginald Cardinal provides humour through his misunderstanding of Stevens's attempts to explain the facts of life to him; this **parodies** the far more serious misunderstandings on the part of Lord Darlington, as well as Stevens and Miss Kenton's misunderstandings of one another. He also tells Stevens about the seriousness of Lord Darlington's involvement with the Nazis and shows a real concern and caring attitude towards Lord Darlington which mirrors that of Stevens. The final **irony** for Reginald Cardinal is that he is killed in Belgium in the Second World War, by the very people Lord Darlington was trying to help; and it is a newspaper, perhaps even the one he worked for (the columns Reginald Cardinal used to write were 'rarely to Lord Darlington's liking', p. 223), that brands Lord Darlington a Nazi sympathiser and brings about his downfall.

The people Stevens encounters during his journey serve primarily to display his attempts and failure to banter, converse and mix with ordinary people. This is partly due to Stevens's own snobbery, and to his secluded life at Darlington Hall, which he has not been away from for a great many years, and also due to the barriers he has erected around himself so as not to be distracted from being a perfect butler like his father and a credit to Lord Darlington. The old man at the start of the journey urges him to see a 'view' which introduces the theme of blindness and seeing (see Themes). It is not, however, a happy encounter, but he has more success with the woman whose chicken he nearly runs over on the way to Salisbury. The woman's warmth puts Stevens in a positive frame of mind to see a view, of Salisbury cathedral, which in turn leads him to remember and reflect on the past. The Taylors are taken in by Stevens's distinguished appearance and together with their neighbours they provide Stevens with the opportunity to 'become' Lord Darlington. Their discussions provide insights into the minds and hearts of ordinary people, people who according to Lord Darlington's fascist beliefs should play no part in politics. As a socialist, Dr Carlisle had opposing views to Lord Darlington, but he points out the hidden apathy of these people despite their big talk. In his view, they actually want to be left alone, which is **ironic**, as it suggests a rejection of both fascism and socialism. Dr Carlisle, though, was willing to live and work amongst the people, and compromised his views, unlike Lord Darlington, who seems remote and cut off from the real world, preferring a world of ideas and ideals which fit in with his beliefs and values, his 'code'. Dr Carlisle is also a true gentleman, who is decent and kind; he sees through Stevens's 'gentleman' act but does not betray him, a stark contrast to the episode involving Mr Spencer, when Stevens is cruelly ridiculed and humiliated.

The retired butler at the end of the novel is another nameless stranger whom Stevens encounters and, like all the others, provides help during Stevens's journey. He opens up a conversation with Stevens using banter and listens sympathetically as Stevens pours out his feelings and grief about his wasted life. He helps him through the pain of facing up to what he has always run away from. He pulls Stevens back from the brink of despair with the wise and reassuring advice that Stevens should relax and enjoy the 'remains of his day' – his old age, the **metaphor** of the novel's title. He is an alter ego for Stevens as he is a retired butler, in a mirror-image of his life, providing a glimpse of how Stevens's life could have been and how it still could be, with a change of attitude. He connects to Mr Benn in this way, as he too was a butler, but realised his limitations and chose a life away from serevice and became self-employed. Mr Benn also recognised and faced his own feelings for Miss Kenton, appreciating her worth and marrying her, although their marriage has been under the strain of the fact that she is not in love with him. He is to retire through ill health but has his old age to look forward to: he will grow old with his wife, and they have a grandchild to look forward to. Through the retired butler and Mr Benn Stevens is shown what he could have had, and what he sacrificed for Lord Darlington and for the sake of being the perfect butler.

THEMES

BANTER

Banter is a central and unifying theme in *The Remains of the Day*. Stevens introduces it in the Prologue as a problem which he considers his duty to solve in order to please Mr Farraday. Stevens takes this new duty very seriously. He ponders over it, practises in his room, and studies a radio programme called *Twice a Week or More* for its witticisms. He practises banter on the people he meets, such as the locals in the Coach and Horses inn near Taunton, but is unsuccessful. He agonises over it yet fails to realise that it is his delivery that is lacking. The true significance of banter becomes apparent at the end of the novel when Stevens has met the retired butler who strikes up a conversation with him and tells him to enjoy his old age. Stevens then listens to the chatter of the people around him, in a positive frame of mind, and realises that banter is 'the key to human warmth'.

Stevens, in his obsession with being the perfect butler, has created so many barriers around himself that he is only able to relate to others as a butler – he cannot relax or be himself. As his journey progresses, however, he begins to lower his barriers and even relaxes enough to join the locals at the Coach and Horses for some cider. He never fully ceases to be Stevens the butler, but his outlook broadens to some extent. At the end of the novel, having faced up to the fact that he has truly wasted his life, he sees the value of bantering and resolves to improve his skills and try harder at it, although he seems to be reserving these potential skills solely for Mr Farraday: he still sees bantering as a duty. Stevens does not seem to entertain the idea of retirement, despite the encouragement of the retired butler. There is thus an ambiguity about banter as the novel closes.

Butlers & dignity

Stevens seems preoccupied with the notion of dignity and the concept of what makes a 'great' butler. He cites his own father as an example of a perfect butler who demonstrated a 'dignity in keeping with one's position' when the drunken gentlemen apologised to him and the General praised him. The key **trope** linked with this theme is the story of the 'tiger under the table', Stevens senior's favourite tale. Stevens seems to be emulating his father and there are several echoes of these incidents, particularly the two occasions when Stevens faces his own 'tiger under the table': when his father dies and when Miss Kenton agrees to marry Mr Benn. When Lord Darlington apologises to Stevens for the behaviour of Mr Spencer we are again reminded of his father.

Stevens has become obsessed, however, and takes being a perfect butler to excess. This can be understood as a reaction to the coldness of his relationship with his father. He has channelled all of his emotions and energies into being the perfect butler, as it gives him a purpose in life and an escape and relief from the empty misery of his unloving relationship with his father. Stevens uses his duty to hide from emotion, such as Miss Kenton's crying, which is threatening to him. He focuses on serving port when his father is dying and when Miss Kenton has agreed to Mr Benn's marriage proposal. He discusses Giffen's silver polish in detail and focuses on it to the exclusion of real life and real events. As a butler, he sees himself as a general drawing up battle plans and believes his small contributions are helping Lord Darlington's political aims – **ironically**, this means helping Lord Darlington with his fascist views, dangerous political moves and ultimately to his downfall. Stevens has almost become his father, even down to the 'errors' he is making at work, which echo his father's errors that Miss Kenton pointed out. When Stevens looks towards his old age, he sees only work, recalling his father in 1923 who died at work – a hauntingly prophetic view of Stevens's own future. Despite his greatness at being a butler, Stevens's father was not too dignified to get married and have two sons. Stevens, however, has denied himself this. Furthermore, his father worked for an industrialist, Mr John Silvers, a fact which precluded him from entry into the Hayes Society. The Hayes Society and life below stairs to some extent reflect and uphold the attitudes of the upper classes: there is a clear hierarchy within the world of servants, which Stevens is at the top of; and there is snobbery amongst the servants about their employers, in the same way that the upper classes embrace those who have inherited land and money and despise those who gain wealth through business. The Hayes Society seems to mirror a Gentlemen's Club. Stevens tries to conceal, but betrays, a degree of bitterness about this club, if not necessarily for himself, then certainly for his father's exclusion from it. Stevens provides warm images of life below stairs in Darlington Hall's heyday, scenes of the employees, including visiting servants, gathered round the fire to debate what makes a 'great' butler, and this underpins the sense of loss Stevens feels in the present of 1956 – with the demise of Lord Darlington and the Hall, there is a demise of the cosy gatherings round the fire and the chance to discuss, debate and share, all of which Stevens enjoyed in the past.

Stevens strongly asserts that he did achieve 'dignity in keeping with one's position' at the end of the Moscombe chapter, when he absolves himself from blame and distances himself from Lord Darlington and his actions. Earlier in this chapter, the topic of dignity crops up in the discussions involving the Taylors and their neighbours. In this case, however, it relates to being a gentleman, and we sense that, since Stevens is pretending to be a gentleman, he feels himself to be on equal terms with gentlemen, and thus with Lord Darlington. Stevens's excessive modesty hides not only his feelings but also pride, vanity and a large ego; he is a human being, not perfect, as he tries to insist. This is what the reader can see, but Stevens cannot, although he comes to face it.

Stevens believes that a butler should '*inhabit* his role, utterly and fully' (p. 178). He believes he must repress his own identity and become a butler to the point of being nothing else. He sacrifices Miss Kenton for his vision of being a perfect butler, and hides behind his job when he cannot cope with reality and emotions. He criticises her in his capacity of butler after her aunt has died, because he is completely unable to relate to her on an honest, human level. He wants to console her and agonises for hours about what to say to her, but he is weak and afraid of emotion, and thus chooses to hide behind his work. He hides his real personality behind the perfect butler persona that he presents to the world. It is often very difficult to maintain this persona – when his father has a stroke and is dying, he refuses to allow it to affect his work, trying not to let on that he is suffering over it; but the depths of pain beneath the apparently calm exterior are revealed by the tears streaming down his face, which only Lord Darlington and Mr Cardinal notice.

It is this same persona that causes Miss Kenton so much frustration. She becomes infuriated and tries to provoke him, especially with her cruel words when Stevens gives no reaction to the news that she is to marry Mr Benn. She desperately wants to get to know Stevens, for him to lower his barriers and reveal the man behind the persona, which could blossom into a real relationship, but he will never allow this.

ENGLISHNESS & AMERICANS

Part of Stevens's identity, which is bound up with Lord Darlington, is being English. He feels that the English countryside reflects the English people, with its 'calmness' and 'sense of restraint', unlike other countries that have 'inferior' sights due to their 'unseemly demonstrativeness' (p. 29). He feels that 'butlers only truly exist in England' as their temperament contains the appropriate 'emotional restraint' (p. 44). This complements the concept of the true English gentleman who possesses a similar restraint, embodying a code of honour and values like decency and fair play. These values and code of honour provide the motivation for Lord Darlington's involvement with fascism, a desire to help Germany after the First World War, and become the focus of Mr Lewis's comments on Lord Darlington being a political 'amateur'.

Mr Lewis, an American, is characterised as being brash, confident and unafraid to voice his opinions and to be unpopular, as well as ruthless in his means of trying to get his own way, with his private talks with M. Dupont. He gives his truthful but insulting judgement on Lord Darlington and refuses to leave the room, unembarrassed by disapproval and censure. M. Dupont seems excessively preoccupied by his blisters, something which makes him seem old, gullible and insipid, despite the importance of his role. His pride and ego are insulted by Mr Lewis's perception that he is being taken in by the scheming English, and he is determined to assert himself. His speech, like that of Mr Lewis, is full of passion and he attacks Mr Lewis. Both speeches are very un-English as they are direct, full of emotion and very much to the point.

Lord Darlington is not, however, a perfect gentleman. He is taken in by the Nazis to a dangerous degree, fires two maids because they are Jewish (although he later regrets it), and subjects Stevens to cruel ridicule by Mr Spencer, which he later apologises for. Kazuo Ishiguro gently pokes fun at his gentlemanly 'emotional restraint' when David Cardinal asks him to speak to Reginald about sex as he is getting married soon. Lord Darlington passes this task on to Stevens, and a comical encounter based on a complete misunderstanding ensues. There is a marked contrast between Mr Farraday's casual bantering with Stevens and Lord Darlington's awkward manner of addressing him. This is described in detail on p. 63, where Stevens explains Lord Darlington's ploy of pretending to consult an encyclopedia, and is summed up neatly on p. 84: 'He seated himself at his desk and, as usual, resorted to holding open a book – this time it was *Who's Who* – turning a page to and fro.'

Mr Farraday is an American and unused to English ways, as Stevens points out in a superior tone in the Prologue. Stevens is not above using this to his advantage, however, as when he explains his denial of working for Lord Darlington to Mr Farraday, after the Wakefields have visited. His seemingly negative attitude to Mr Farraday in the Prologue could be because his opinion of Americans was formed by his experience of Mr Lewis in 1923, a man whom Stevens felt was 'duplicitous' (p. 90). Furthermore, at this point Lord Darlington has died only three years earlier, and Stevens is clearly still suffering from this. He is unused to his new employer and struggling with the errors that have started appearing in his work. He faces what these errors signify at the end of the novel – that he has given his all to Lord Darlington – but they are also reminiscent of his own father's errors that Miss Kenton pointed out. Stevens appears to have changed his attitude to Mr Farraday by the end of the novel, resolving to banter with him in future and practise it so he can surprise him on his return to the Hall.

HUMOUR & STEVENS'S 'LAUGH'

Kazuo Ishiguro punctures the quiet tragedy of the novel with moments of supreme humour. Stevens is not remotely aware of any of this humour. This links to the three-fold perspective in the novel, whereby there is Stevens's perspective on events, the reader's and, ultimately, the author's (see Narrative Techniques). Ishiguro pokes fun at his creation, Stevens, in a gentle way, by **satirising** the way he takes himself so seriously. This satire appears, for example, when Ishiguro describes Stevens studying a witty radio programme entitled *Twice a Week or More* and having 'devised a simple exercise ... to formulate three witticisms based on my immediate surroundings' (p. 139). It also appears when Stevens attempts to banter with the locals at the Coach and Horses and they do not immediately laugh (p. 138), and again with Mr Farraday over a crowing noise (p. 17). The reader is also amused when Mr Farraday teases Stevens about 'a lady-friend' and when Stevens agonises over the fork that Mr Farraday idly picks up and looks at during breakfast one morning. Ishiguro even gently mocks the battle of wills between Miss Kenton and Stevens when she insists that he view an incorrectly placed Chinaman, and he refuses, remaining trapped in the billiard room and contemplating escape from her 'via the french windows'. The effect of the humour is to emphasise that Stevens takes himself too seriously, and furthermore, that he has lost his sense of humour. He does not see anything funny in these episodes, as he is concentrating so much on being perfect. He never laughs in the novel – except as a disguise (part of his persona), to hide what he is really feeling, which is usually the opposite of laughing. At the end of his meeting with Miss Kenton, he noticeably hides his heartbreak with a smile. A variation on his enigmatic smile and laugh is a cough, used, for example, when discussing Harry Smith's views with Dr Carlisle (p. 219).

Ishiguro capitalises on the misunderstanding between Stevens and Reginald Cardinal regarding the facts of life and a love of nature, and juxtaposes the humour of this against the backdrop of the tensions of the 1923 conference and Stevens's father's death. Stevens does not see the humour in his encounter with Mr Cardinal, from the moment he emerges from a bush and startles him, to his words, 'If I may come straight to the point' (p. 93). Clearly, Stevens does not come straight to the point, and a bewildered Mr Cardinal thinks that Stevens is interested in geese and foliage. Again, the humour is gently mocking, and adds a poignancy to the tragic events as they unfold, as Mr Cardinal reminds Stevens of their conversation, when Stevens's father has died and he is trying to hide his grief. Ishiguro skilfully underlines the emptiness of Stevens's choice of duty to Lord Darlington over his own father with this incident, but Stevens fails to see it and does not learn from it, either at the time or in 1956. This is echoed by a similar juxtaposition in 1936 when Mr Cardinal reappears just as Miss Kenton has agreed to marry Mr Benn, when Herr Ribbentrop, the Prime Minister and the Foreign Secretary are meeting secretly at Darlington Hall.

SEEING & BLINDNESS

Stevens is so focused on being a perfect butler to the exclusion of all else, including world events, that he does not see reality and truth. If the truth does not fit in with his vision and ambitions, he does not want to see it. He does not mention the Suez Crisis of 1956 (see Historical Background), but instead spends two pages or so discussing Giffen's silver polish. He feels it is more important for him to serve port to the gentlemen than to be with his dying father. Mr Cardinal tells him categorically in 1936 that Lord Darlington is mistaken with his political ideals of fascism, but Stevens refuses to believe it. His eyes, heart and emotions are focused completely on his vision of himself as the perfect butler serving the perfect man. Consequently he also does not see that Miss Kenton loves him – he is blind to her moods and silences. He attempts to analyse them, but comes to the wrong conclusions, dismissing Mr Graham, who can see what is really wrong with her, namely that she is getting older and longs for a family of her own. Stevens is in denial about all issues that do not form part of his vision, and he is also in denial about the fact that he has wasted his life on a man who was not perfect. This is what he psychologically journeys to face, recalling memories on the way, but pulling back from them when they become too painful or uncomfortable.

  Stevens is helped by the people he meets on his car journey; they provide physical assistance with the car and, by directing him to see beautiful views, they also help him to face the past. The views **symbolise** the act of seeing clearly and they provide respite from travelling. As Stevens travels, **literally** and **metaphorically**, he needs time to rest and these moments lead him to reflect on his life and begin to face what he has been unable to face until now. Stevens is contemptuous of what he calls a 'mindless sort of "loyalty"' (p. 210), but he demonstrates it himself with his blindness to Lord Darlington's flaws, even refusing to take in Mr Cardinal's words when he openly tells Stevens of Lord Darlington's political folly. This refusal to face things is part of Stevens's blindness, which is partly self-imposed and partly weakness on his part.

The themes of seeing and blindness connect to the novel's **images** of light and dark (see also Imagery & Symbolism). The lights on the pier in Weymouth coincide with Stevens's ability to see his life clearly and positively for the first time, coming to accept its waste and lack of dignity. Stevens walks up a dark passage to fetch port for the gentlemen when Miss Kenton has accepted Mr Benn's proposal, and the darkness **symbolises** all that is wrong with Stevens's life – his blindness, stubbornness and refusal to see anything except his vision and sacrifice for Lord Darlington. Miss Kenton has light in her room, a symbol of truth, reality, hope and love; Stevens hesitates but walks away from this. They sit in mist and darkness in the summerhouse, an environment which suggests their misunderstanding and lack of communication. He does not see her love for him, while she does not see or understand his obsession and his vision. And in 1956, Stevens has an uncomfortable insight into a lonely, dark and sterile old age in the **pathetic fallacy** of the darkness on the lonely hill: 'it was not a happy feeling to be up there on a lonely hill, looking … at the lights coming on in a distant village, the daylight all but faded, and the mist growing ever thicker' (p. 170). Stevens is **metaphorically** on a dark, lonely hill of his own making, having cut himself off from humanity as part of his quest for perfection, which proved to be a futile exercise. All he is left with is darkness and loneliness, unless he reaches out to others, using banter.

TRIVIALITY

Interlinked with the themes of banter and dignity is the idea that apparently trivial things reveal things of greater significance. Stevens himself introduces this theme and attributes the words 'These errors may be trivial in themselves, but you must yourself realize their larger significance' first to Miss Kenton (pp. 61–2) and then to Lord Darlington (p. 63). In both cases they are talking about the errors in his father's work, the kind of errors which Stevens himself makes in 1956, when working for Mr Farraday. As well as suggesting that the reader cannot take everything Stevens says at face value (see Narrative Techniques), his uncertainty here also shows that he has muddled the two most important people in his life, to the point that he can no longer reliably distinguish between them.

Stevens deliberately chooses to focus upon what is trivial as a means of ensuring he attains perfect butler status and maintaining his persona. He finds emotions and uncomfortable situations too much to cope with, so he hides behind his work, choosing to serve port when his father is dying in 1923 and again in 1936 when Miss Kenton has decided to marry Mr Benn. In real terms, it is immaterial whether he or another employee serves the port, but in Stevens's frame of reference, he alone must do it; not to do so would constitute a lack of perfection, and would also mean having to face uncomfortable and painful events. He spends time dealing with minutiae, such as whether or not Miss Kenton should address his father as 'William', and the wonders of Giffen's silver polish, but he refuses to or cannot see that Lord Darlington is gravely mistaken in his political views and that Miss Kenton loves him. He never mentions world events, simply because they serve no purpose in contributing to his vision. He instead focuses completely on his work and on Lord Darlington, even telling Reginald Cardinal in 1936 that he has failed to notice Adolf Hitler and the rise of the Nazis in Germany. Focusing on trivialities is Stevens's way of escaping from truth and reality and protecting himself from pain.

SYMBIOSIS

'Symbiosis' is a word which can be used to describe an interdependent relationship between two people, which is mutually advantageous. Lord Darlington needs Stevens to run Darlington Hall efficiently, and on the simplest level Stevens needs Lord Darlington to need him as a butler. However, Stevens's needs transcend the limits of their symbiotic relationship in both depth and complexity. His blind faith in Lord Darlington and unswerving devotion to serve him in the best way possible resemble an almost religious fervour. Stevens centres his whole life around Lord Darlington - serving him is his entire raison d'être. Stevens has been starved of love and affection by his father. He denies his own emotions and needs in order to try to be a perfect butler like him; imitation is, proverbially, the highest form of flattery. Stevens was trained by his father when he was a young man, and this was perhaps the greatest amount of attention he ever received from his father.

Stevens's emotions are channelled into his hero-worship of Lord Darlington. He is obsessed with Lord Darlington to an almost religious extent – indeed, Stevens seems to revere and follow Lord Darlington like a disciple worshipping and following Jesus Christ (see Imagery & Symbolism). He is blind to his employer's faults or justifies them, choosing to believe only the best about him. He sacrifices his one chance of love for the sake of Lord Darlington, and **ironically**, was wasting his time, as Lord Darlington's fascist beliefs were his undoing. At the Taylors' home, Stevens is mistaken for a gentleman and decides to play along; for a brief time, he becomes Lord Darlington, the man he has served and worshipped. Symbiosis progresses to imitation and ultimately here to impersonation. It seems that with both his role models, Stevens cannot help but imitate them - especially when they are no longer there to need him. But by facing and accepting the past during his psychological journey, Stevens gradually frees himself from what has become the grip of these past relationships.

IMAGERY & SYMBOLISM

CLOTHING & APPEARANCES

Stevens discusses clothes on a **literal** level in the Prologue, when he expresses his concern about what to wear on his journey. He reveals he owns suits passed on to him from Lord Darlington and various guests, and that his concern is to be appropriately attired as a representative and butler of Darlington Hall. Clothes have a further **symbolic** meaning, as they connect to the persona of the perfect butler. This persona is like a mask that Stevens wears all the time; he represses his own identity, thoughts and feelings, in order to preserve 'dignity in keeping with one's position'. He says and believes that 'A butler of any quality must be seen to *inhabit* his role, utterly and fully; he cannot be seen casting it aside ... as though it were nothing more than a pantomime costume' (p. 178). He even remains a butler when he is 'off-duty', in his pantry and while alone in the guest house in Salisbury waiting for his tea. He never relaxes and never takes a day off. He even describes dignity to Dr Carlisle in terms of clothes: 'it comes down to not removing one's clothing in public' (p. 221).

Clothing also connects to the world of objects that Stevens inhabits and the way he continually anticipates criticism from the reader. As a butler, Stevens can be judged in terms of his performance and the objects he is in charge of at any time: he exists in a world of surfaces and objects that must be cleaned and cared for, and thus presentation and outward show are all-important. Stevens himself embraces this; there may be Nazism and anti-Semitism in Darlington Hall, but, more importantly to Stevens, the silverware is seen to be impressive. His professional and personal worlds are one and the same; he is paid to maintain the appearance of the house and he himself tries to maintain a perfectly smooth exterior. He does not want to look beyond the surface in terms of life, events and people because they are too threatening to him, so he hides behind his work. The persona does slip from time to time during the novel so that Stevens's true feelings can be seen, but the reader has to read between the lines to grasp when it is Stevens's persona talking and when it is the 'real' Stevens (see also Narrative Techniques).

Stevens wears Lord Darlington's clothes that have been handed down to him, and there are occasions when he is mistaken for a real gentleman, by locals en route, and particularly the Taylors, although the chauffeur and Dr Carlisle see what he really is, a butler. The retired butler in Weymouth does not realise that Stevens is a butler until Stevens tells him. Yet he is not intimidated by Stevens and strikes up a conversation with him using banter, anyway. He says: 'Just shows you never know who you're addressing when you start talking to a stranger' (p. 254).

STEVENS'S JOURNEY

Stevens drives from Oxfordshire to Cornwall in Mr Farraday's car over six days, but his journey is also a **metaphorical**, psychological one. Until this journey, he has evaded and been unable to face certain fundamental truths about his life. **Ironically**, it is only by leaving Darlington Hall – his psychological 'prison' (see Doors on p. 83 of this Note) – that Stevens will truly be able to see, and then reflect upon, his life at the Hall. He is in denial over these fundamental truths but must turn to face them if he is to make any changes in his life, so that he can enjoy the remains of his day, his old age, as the retired butler suggests. He cannot face the fact that he has lost the love of his life, Miss Kenton, or that the man he sacrificed her for, and indeed his whole life for, was ultimately not worth it. Equally, he cannot face the fact that he is not a perfect butler and has not attained the greatness and dignity he pretends that he has. All of these situations have come about through decisions he has made himself. Mr Cardinal told Stevens in 1936 that Lord Darlington was mistaken in his political views but Stevens would not listen. Miss Kenton tried for years to get to know the real Stevens behind the persona, but he would not allow it. He preferred to live in his own world, in his own vision of himself as the perfect butler serving the perfect man. These views and this vision are expressed during the journey and the reader is not fully aware of the precise nature of certain events but must wait for details to unfold. Stevens's mental journey begins with memories of the past that he presents to the reader and is sometimes able to analyse. He is helped by people on his journey, who direct him to see beautiful views that trigger memories or aid contemplation. At the end of the novel, Stevens has made sufficient headway to be able to face the reality of his wasted life and try to accept it, to put it behind him and look forward to the future.

THE FALL MOTIF

All of the main characters and some of the minor ones suffer a fall in some way during the novel. It is a **motif** which connects the characters. The first fall is a **literal** one, that of Stevens's father, which anticipates his fatal stroke during the conference in 1923. Lisa and the second footman fall in love – this mirrors the love Miss Kenton has for Stevens and acts as a catalyst for her longing for love, romance and a family of her own. Miss Kenton's own fall is one of 'pride before a fall' in her faith in Lisa, having taken her under her wing in the face of Stevens's opposition. David Cardinal falls from a horse and is killed in a riding accident and Reginald Cardinal falls in battle in Belgium during the Second World War. Lord Darlington suffers a fall from grace when he unsuccessfully sues a newspaper for libel after the Second World War. Stevens has the potential to fall into despair as he faces his wasted life on the pier at Weymouth; but he is saved by the retired butler, who offers him hope, and instead hears the people around himself 'fall into conversation with one another' (p. 257).

BIBLICAL REFERENCES

The biblical references in *The Remains of the Day* are implicit and centre around Stevens's worship of Lord Darlington as a disciple worshipping Jesus Christ. At one point Stevens says: 'The day his lordship's work is complete ... only on that day ... will I be able to call myself ... a well-contented man' (p. 182). The words and tone of this speech are almost religious, and Stevens certainly sees himself as Lord Darlington's helper. By ensuring that things proceed smoothly in the house, such as the excellence in silver polish, Stevens believes he is helping political matters to go smoothly for Lord Darlington. The **irony** of this – which Stevens cannot see, either at the time or in 1956 – is that he is helping with Lord Darlington's downfall. Stevens, like the disciple Peter who denies Christ in the New Testament Book of Mark (Chapter 14, verses 66–72), denies Lord Darlington three times. He denies working for Lord Darlington when speaking to the chauffeur and to the Wakefields, and denies his involvement with Lord Darlington when addressing the reader at the end of the Moscombe chapter. In biblical terms, he becomes like Pontius Pilate here, too. Pontius Pilate was the Roman Governor to whom Jesus was brought when he was arrested. Pilate washed his hands of Jesus (**literally** and **metaphorically**) by handing him back to the Jews to be killed and allowing them a free reign in their actions over this. Stevens, at the end of the Moscombe chapter, absolves himself of guilt over Lord Darlington's ruin, denies him and distances himself from him and his activities, to the point of saying, 'It is hardly my fault if his lordship's life and work have turned out today to look, at best, a sad waste' (p. 211).

The fall **motif** (see above) can also be extended to Adam and Eve's fall from the Garden of Eden. In the novel, Darlington Hall in its heyday can be compared to Eden and the fall is represented by Lord Darlington's ruin and its impact on Stevens. Stevens has in some sense been cast out of Eden and cannot find salvation until the retired butler at Weymouth offers him hope for a happy future.

Miss Kenton uses a biblical word, 'sin' (p. 157), to describe Lord Darlington's dismissal of the Jewish maids, a word with a meaning which goes beyond simply doing something wrong. It suggests, in Christian terms, that it is wrong to the point of staining one's soul and that one will have to face up to it in the afterlife and receive punishment. Lord Darlington is not as morally good as Stevens portrays him, and he is clearly not furthering humanity with his Nazi links, but doing the opposite.

Hands

Hands are a **symbol** in the novel of one's life's work and achievement, centring around Stevens's father and Miss Kenton. When Stevens senior is dying, after checking that events in the house are 'in hand' (p. 101), he looks at his hands 'With some deliberation' for some time and asks whether he has been a good father to Stevens, which Stevens does not answer. He tells him he is proud of his son and seems 'faintly irritated' by his hands. Stevens's father, on his deathbed, is looking back over his life and thinking of his achievements. He has achieved a great deal in his work, but his relationship with his son is a failure. Indeed, they have no real relationship, and there is a coldness between them to the point that Stevens addresses his father in the third person. Stevens senior's life and work are thus a mixture of success and failure, which he faces and expresses as he looks at his hands.

Miss Kenton also looks at her hands when despairing over Lisa's departure (p. 166). The young woman has reminded her of her own age and the emptiness in her life, that the years are passing her by and she has made no progress with Stevens; Stevens states that he 'cannot really recall seeing her more bereft than on that morning'. She is at a turning point in her life: she could remain alone and unfulfilled in the Hall or try to make things work with Stevens, or with someone else. This is compounded when she is deciding whether or not to marry Mr Benn. She is in her parlour and 'there was nothing before her and her hands were empty' (p. 224). By now she knows for sure that there will never be a future for her with Stevens, but she is reluctant to take such a big step and walk away from him. When he gives her no reaction, she looks back at her hands (p. 225) as though to remind herself that she must act, that she must accept Mr Benn. Her work is no longer fulfilling; she craves love, affection and a family, and Stevens will never provide these things. She has no ring on her finger and no baby to hold. Her hands symbolise all she lacks and hopes for and they help her to make up her mind.

LIGHT & DARK

Darkness is a metaphor for the state of Stevens's relationship with Miss Kenton and for their misunderstandings and lack of communication. Stevens's pantry is dark, as Miss Kenton notices on p. 54 when she wants to 'brighten' his room up. Each battle of wills occurs during a dark afternoon, either due to the weather or in dark corridors (for example, p. 82). The kitchen is dark when she has accepted Mr Benn (p. 228). Stevens rejects Miss Kenton in the dark summerhouse when she has declared that she could not leave Darlington Hall as she would find 'nobody who knew or cared about me' if she left, by which she means Stevens (p. 161). She becomes infuriated by him, demanding, 'Why, Mr Stevens, why, why, why do you always have to *pretend*?' (p. 162), seeing, but not fully understanding, his persona – the mist and darkness around the summerhouse symbolise the fact that they do not understand each other. The corridor is dark when Stevens fetches the port after Miss Kenton has accepted Mr Benn. Miss Kenton, by contrast, is in her room full of light (p. 237), symbolising warmth, hope and love, but Stevens remains in the dark, devoid of hope and possibility.

 Stevens generally seems comfortable in the dark, but this changes during his journey as he sees his lonely and isolated position in its true misery as he stands on a dark, misty, lonely hill looking at the comforting and warm lights of the nearby village (p. 170). Here, darkness connects to the metaphor of the remains of one's day (old age), before night (death) approaches. Stevens has no comforting evening to look forward to, but is urged to enjoy the remains of his day by the retired butler in Weymouth, who helps Stevens avoid despair at his wasted life. The lights come on as Stevens sits on the pier: as he pulls himself back from the brink of despair, choosing to try to accept his life instead, the 'light has dawned' at last for Stevens.

DOORS

Stevens is in a psychological 'prison', one which he has created with his persona and the repression of his feelings. Darlington Hall, and in particular his pantry, is a **metaphor** for this prison. As Stevens's life is spent primarily indoors, open and closed doors become further indicators of the state of his relationship with Miss Kenton and **symbolise** the barriers he has created around himself. Miss Kenton tries to break down these barriers by going into his pantry to introduce flowers into the room, to be friendly and personal, but Stevens resists this.

Miss Kenton's territory is her parlour, from which she emerges to chastise Stevens and into which she then withdraws (at pp. 58–9, for example). She waits outside the door to the billiard room over the issue of the misplaced Chinaman. She is often in a doorway, a threshold, unsure of herself – this can be seen as a parallel to her life, as she is in a state of limbo with regard to Stevens. Following the death of his father and as the years progress, they meet on neutral territory, for example in the summerhouse. She even persuades him to join her for cocoa in her parlour, a sign of the cordiality and warmth between them, which she mistakes for something more, but which he only sees as a professional meeting.

Arguably the most significant door is the one between Stevens and Miss Kenton when he hesitates outside, convinced that she is crying. This can be understood as both a **literal** and a **metaphorical** door – it represents a closed door in his mind which he fails to open, just as he fails to open the physical door to her room. As an unreliable **narrator** (see Narrative Techniques), he mistakes this occasion, but subsequently corrects himself. Miss Kenton emerges 'at the threshold' (p. 236) of her parlour and of her new life without Stevens. It is Stevens's last chance to stop her from marrying Mr Benn. She lowers her barriers in the form of an apology to Stevens, which he receives ungraciously, conveying to her that she means nothing to him. She then closes her door, closing all hope of a future and a life with Stevens.

Stevens sees things clearly outside where there are no doors during his journey, and thus he is open and honest with the butler on Weymouth pier. By this point, all doors and his barriers have disappeared. (See also Place & Time.)

TIREDNESS

This is Stevens's device for explaining away his emotions to Lord Darlington: 'The strains of a hard day' (p. 110). It is a sign of great emotional turbulence that may not be immediately apparent – in fact, the tiredness is its only symptom. Miss Kenton describes herself as 'tired' after she is rejected by Stevens (p. 183), and is feeling the full impact of that pain. He later echoes her words when she not only agrees to marry Mr Benn but cruelly tells him that they mock and ridicule him. It is Mr Cardinal who notices that Stevens appears to be ill and Stevens explains he is 'tired', in an echo of the aftermath of his father dying. Stevens also uses this word at the end of the novel to explain to the reader why he has remained the extra night in Weymouth. It becomes apparent, though, that he is still reeling from his encounter with Miss Kenton to the point that Day Five is omitted from the **narrative** altogether; it is as though it takes him a full day to get over their meeting before being able to resume and finish his narration (see also Place & Time). She expressed her love for him and his heart broke at her words and at the realisation that he sacrificed her, for nothing. As he cries to the retired butler, he again explains himself as being 'tired', and again it is clear that he is in emotional turmoil as he faces up to the fact that he has wasted his life. The retired butler sees that Stevens is crying and offers help and support. Stevens is now tired of his persona and lowers all barriers, becoming himself at last.

OBJECTS

Stevens, as butler, is concerned with the care and presentation of objects. Some of these take on a **symbolic** meaning within the novel. For example, Miss Kenton describes Stevens's father as searching for a 'precious jewel' outside the summerhouse (p. 52). The jewel can be understood as a **metaphor** for his dignity, which he has lost, never to regain, due to his fall.

A person's private room is in some ways an expression and projection of their personality and it is appropriate that Ishiguro depicts the rooms of both Stevens and his father as prison cells. They have locked themselves in emotional prisons and sacrificed fulfilling relationships – Stevens with Miss Kenton, and Stevens senior with his son.

Miss Kenton, on the other hand, is associated with flowers, **symbols** of colour, warmth, vitality and life. She wants to 'brighten' up Stevens's dark prison cell of a pantry, but he rejects it. Her fiery personality certainly brightens up his life and yet, like a living flower, she needs care and attention, things which Stevens will not provide her with. The romantic novel she finds him reading symbolises what Stevens denies himself in life: warmth, comfort, love and care. It is as though he is trying to find out about the very things he will not allow himself; the book is a window into a world he will never enter, and it is **ironic** that Miss Kenton, who finds him with it, does in fact love him. He reads about love but does not recognise it when it is **literally** and **metaphorically** right in front of him.

NARRATIVE TECHNIQUES

THE UNRELIABLE NARRATOR

The sole **narrative** voice in *The Remains of the Day* is that of Stevens. He talks about himself and his life, sharing it with the reader. During the narrative he lowers the barriers he has created around himself and faces the truth about his life that he has hitherto been unable to face. He is, however, at times unreliable as a **narrator**. As the sole speaker, the reader must accept Stevens's version of events. There is no corroborating evidence, although there are references to real people, such as Lord Halifax, Winston Churchill and Herr Ribbentrop, which lend an authenticity to the narrative. Stevens is unreliable as he is dependent on his memory, a memory that is selective and chooses to forget things, or not to see things, or that is biased. Examples of this occur when he muddles Miss Kenton and Lord Darlington over the comment about errors being trivial but signifying something more and when he is confused about when exactly he hesitated outside Miss Kenton's room as she was crying. There are other occasions that are more subtle, such as his insistence on the fact that he wants to see Miss Kenton for 'professional' reasons, when the reader learns at the end that he loves her. He portrays Miss Kenton as wanting to return to the Hall (p. 50) and later admits that he has read too much into her letter (p. 189). There is the implicit suggestion that Lord Darlington was not the sort of employer whose butler was 'displayed as a kind of performing monkey' (p. 36), yet we learn later that Stevens was summoned to answer the questions of

Mr Spencer, although he declined, and was used to demonstrate a point. Stevens insists during the narrative that Lord Darlington was an innocent bystander to fascism, but Mr Cardinal reveals the extent of his involvement, that he was trying to persuade the Prime Minister and the King to have stronger ties with Hitler. Hence the reader cannot take what Stevens says at face value and must think carefully about what is being presented as it may be changed later, or at least, may not be quite as Stevens portrays it.

PRE-EMPTIVE TACTICS

Another of Stevens's quirks as **narrator** is that he is constantly pre-empting criticism. He seems to anticipate it at every turn, for example when he writes, 'you will perhaps excuse my impropriety in referring to her as I knew her' (p. 50), over his use of 'Miss Kenton' to refer to Mrs Benn in his **narrative**. He justifies himself with regard to his treatment of his declining father (p. 73) and is at pains to excuse himself about allowing the car to run out of petrol (p. 168). This could suggest that he is expecting criticism from the implied reader, the 'you' he refers to, or that it is part of his butler's identity. As a butler, he is constantly under scrutiny in his behaviour and performance. He is responsible for objects that must be polished and cleaned and therefore presentation and outward show are important. He can be criticised at any time by his employer, and he also demands perfection of himself. An example of this is when Mr Farraday idly looks at a fork one morning at breakfast, which Stevens interprets as criticism, that there is something wrong with the fork. He removes and replaces the fork, startling Mr Farraday, who, the reader feels, may have intended no criticism at all. Yet Stevens expects perfection of himself and the objects he is in charge of at all times, including at breakfast. Perhaps it is no wonder that he seems on edge in his narrative and continually anticipates criticism, a habit of his connected with his role as butler and the way he 'inhabits' that role.

THREE POINTS OF VIEW

Stevens, as an unreliable **narrator** with an implied reader, has his own perspective on events, that is tied up with his own inability to face the truth. He is biased in favour of Lord Darlington, and plays down his anti-Semitism, but later denounces him and distances himself from him. The actual reader of the text has a separate perspective on Stevens and on the events portrayed. It is a psychological journey, but the reader is in no position to counsel or support Stevens as he faces the truth, as a therapist might in real life; the people he meets en route have to suffice as his 'helpers'.

The reader remains a spectator to Stevens's mental flounderings and learns to be circumspect about what Stevens writes. It is necessary to read carefully as Stevens presents biased and incorrect information as he struggles with himself. The reader can silently disagree with Stevens, for example over the dismissal of the Jewish maids which he insists is insignificant, when it is actually a disgusting abuse of power. The reader is often put in the position of siding with Miss Kenton; in the case of the Jewish maids, Stevens displayed no reaction to these events, no questioning of Lord Darlington over his decision, but later says to Miss Kenton that he was upset about it. She, like the reader, is surprised to hear this and the reader can perhaps share her frustration over Stevens's inability to be himself and show his emotions. The reader, then, has a tenuous relationship with the character of Stevens, and can only remain silent. Stevens is on his own as he remembers the past, his ultimate loneliness.

The third perspective is that of the author, Kazuo Ishiguro. He has constructed and crafted Stevens's **narrative**, has **empathised** with his creation, and formed the mental journey. He is generally unobtrusive in the narration, except perhaps for the novel's moments of humour – for example, Stevens's efforts at bantering in the mirror, to Mr Farraday and to the locals at the Coach and Horses, and his attempts to explain the facts of life to Reginald Cardinal. Stevens appears to have no sense of humour and sees nothing funny in moments like these, which reveal Ishiguro gently poking fun at his creation. Stevens, who takes himself so seriously, has his stern façade punctured unwittingly by the humour in the novel, and Ishiguro deliberately juxtaposes these moments against the growing tragedy, thereby adding to its **pathos**.

THE IMAGINED READER

During Stevens's **narrative** he frequently addresses an implied reader as 'you'. There are several clues as to who 'you' might be and it becomes apparent that Stevens is talking to a fellow servant. He says, 'you will no doubt appreciate how uncomfortable a situation this was for me' (p. 14) when Mr Farraday teases him about having a 'lady-friend'. He goes on to be more specific and talks of 'those such as you and me' and 'the likes of you and I' (pp. 209, 211, 257), indicating that Stevens is addressing an equal who is not a gentleman. He could be talking to his own father in a posthumous gesture to connect with him once again, now that his symbiotic relationship with Lord Darlington is over. The way he anticipates and pre-empts criticism during the novel could suggest this also, as he was originally trained by his father and must have felt his watchful, critical eye upon himself, carrying it with him as he tried to emulate his father and become 'perfect' like him. The narrative could be for the retired butler who saves him from despair at the end of the novel, or it could even be aimed at Miss Kenton. He loves her but never tells her, although he admits it to the reader, when he says how his heart breaks when she tells him she loves him. She was meant for him and her personality complemented his. They were a strong team at work and could have been a strong team in life, but he pushed her away. Perhaps the novel is an extended apology to her and his way of lowering his barriers, finally, to show her the 'real' Stevens and to try to make it up to her.

PLACE & TIME

The novel has a dual time scheme. The 'present day' in the novel begins in July 1956, and involves Stevens driving from Oxfordshire through Salisbury to Cornwall. The novel ends with his stay in Weymouth during the return journey, with the prospect of driving back to Darlington Hall the next day. The journey takes place over six days and Stevens describes each stage and the people he meets en route. The journey is also a psychological one for Stevens, as he faces the past and truths about his life that he has been unable to face before. The views **metaphorically** help him to 'see' aspects of his life and ponder them, just as the people provide opportunities for Stevens to banter with varying degrees of success. The people also help him in **literal** ways with the Ford, for example when it runs out of petrol and water.

The places Stevens visits also connect with the notion of 'Englishness', something that Stevens is preoccupied with (see Themes on Englishness & Americans). The places seem to become more and more stereotypically English as the story progresses. This connects to the images of England that Stevens enjoys in Mrs Symons's *The Wonder of England* as described on p. 12 of the novel. For example, Stevens encounters a picturesque village, where the Taylors live in a cottage in which Mrs Taylor serves broth with crusty bread, and an inn which is a thatched-roof cottage where cider is served in tankards. The author is deliberately conjuring pictures of 'traditional' England to lend authenticity to Stevens's **literal** journey, whilst playing upon unconsciously embedded perceptions of 'Englishness'. Ishiguro has included ideals and removed historical realities, for example the turmoil of Edward VIII's abdication in 1936 and the Suez Crisis that would have been dominating events in England in 1956 – see the Chronology on p. 112 of this Note to compare historical events alongside the events of the novel. Because Stevens is the **narrator,** this tells us a great deal about him. He is clinging to these ideals and ignoring world events around him. He is selective about what he narrates to the reader, and his lack of acknowledgement of world events indicates the extent of his obsession with being a perfect butler and his worship of Lord Darlington – they are described to the exclusion of all else.

Stevens describes not only his journey to Cornwall, but also various memories of the past. The novel includes several **flashbacks,** the earliest of which takes place in spring 1922, when Stevens's father and Miss Kenton arrive at Darlington Hall to work. These flashbacks occur at various intervals in chronological order, moving on to the conference of 1923 and leading into the 1930s. They culminate with Miss Kenton's decision to marry Mr Benn in 1936, which causes her to leave the Hall.

The amount of time Stevens spends describing or discussing an incident can be indicative of the extent to which he is revealing his true feelings. In the Prologue, for example, Stevens spends several pages explaining the reasons behind his faulty staff rota, but only mentions

Miss Kenton's letter in passing, despite the fact that it is the motivation for his journey, and despite the depth of his feelings for her (which we learn of later). The lengthy explanation is a sign of Stevens's persona firmly in place, especially as he insists that he has only a 'professional' interest in Miss Kenton. This lends weight to the argument that the brevity of his description of the Jewish maids' dismissal is evidence of hidden emotions, especially when we consider that Day Five, the day he meets Miss Kenton, is missing from the **narrative** altogether. It is the culmination of his journey and an emotional turning point in his life, and the fact that he does not describe the day's events until Day Six suggests that he requires a day to recover from its impact. This is perhaps the clearest indicator to the reader that the amount of time Stevens devotes to incidents in his narrative merits careful consideration.

It is helpful to consider all the places in Stevens's **narrative** in terms of whether he is inside a building or outside: the places serve as indicators of his progress in facing the psychological truths he has previously hidden from. Being inside a building usually means that Stevens can hide firmly behind his persona, whereas when he is outdoors, he 'sees' his life clearly, as well as the views in front of him. Thus it is not by coincidence that inside the Rose Garden Hotel Stevens engages in news and small talk with Miss Kenton, whereas outside, while waiting for the bus, Miss Kenton declares her feelings and Stevens's heart breaks. Later, Stevens is outside on the pier when he faces up to what his life has become, and confides openly in the retired butler.

PART FOUR

TEXTUAL ANALYSIS

TEXT 1 (PAGES 13–15)

This passage occurs near the start of the Prologue and it introduces the theme of banter, 'a conversation of a light-hearted, humorous sort', which Stevens is incapable of. This is partly due to the nature of his job, but also due to the emotional barriers he has placed around himself. Stevens pre-empts criticism and justifies himself, as he does throughout the novel. He explains that the conversation is his own fault (because he mentions a delicate subject at a time when Farraday likes to banter), as though he is expecting, or at least allowing for the possibility of, the criticism that he should have realised that this was the wrong moment to broach the subject. At the end of this passage, Stevens stresses that he is not suggesting that Farraday was to blame for the embarrassing conversation – again, as though he is aware that he could be criticised for this. It is **ironic** that someone who is at pains to be clearly understood seriously misunderstands others, such as Miss Kenton, to a life-changing degree. Stevens often addresses the reader with the word 'you', as he does here. Who the 'you' is, though, is another matter (see Narrative Techniques).

> As it was, I believe my judgement proved quite sound on the question of timing; the fact that things turned out as they did is entirely attributable to an error of judgement in another direction altogether. That is to say, I did not take sufficient account of the fact that at that time of the day, what Mr Farraday enjoys is a conversation of a light-hearted, humorous sort. Knowing this to be his likely mood when I brought in the tea yesterday afternoon, and being aware of his general propensity to talk with me in a bantering tone at such moments, it would certainly have been wiser not to have mentioned Miss Kenton at all. But you will perhaps understand that there was a natural tendency on my part, in asking what was after all a generous favour from my employer, to hint that there was a good professional motive behind my request. So it was that in indicating my reasons for preferring the West Country for my motoring, instead of leaving it at mentioning several of the alluring details as conveyed by Mrs Symons's volume, I made the error of

declaring that a former housekeeper of Darlington Hall was resident in that region. I suppose I must have been intending to explain to Mr Farraday how I would thus be able to explore an option which might prove the ideal solution to our present small problems here in this house. It was only after I had mentioned Miss Kenton that I suddenly realized how entirely inappropriate it would be for me to continue. Not only was I unable to be certain of Miss Kenton's desire to rejoin the staff here, I had not, of course, even discussed the question of additional staff with Mr Farraday since that first preliminary meeting over a year ago. To have continued pronouncing aloud my thoughts on the future of Darlington Hall would have been, to say the very least, presumptuous. I suspect, then, that I paused rather abruptly and looked a little awkward. In any case, Mr Farraday seized the opportunity to grin broadly at me and say with some deliberation:

'My, my, Stevens. A lady-friend. And at your age.'

This was a most embarrassing situation, one in which Lord Darlington would never have placed an employee. But then I do not mean to imply anything derogatory about Mr Farraday; he is, after all, an American gentleman and his ways are often very different. There is no question at all that he meant any harm; but you will no doubt appreciate how uncomfortable a situation this was for me.

'I'd never have figured you for such a lady's man, Stevens,' he went on. 'Keeps the spirit young, I guess. But then I really don't know it's right for me to be helping you with such dubious assignations.'

Naturally I felt the temptation to deny immediately and unambiguously such motivations as my employer was imputing to me, but saw in time that to do so would be to rise to Mr Farraday's bait, and the situation would only become increasingly embarrassing. I therefore continued to stand there awkwardly, waiting for my employer to give me permission to undertake the motoring trip.

Embarrassing as those moments were for me, I would not wish to imply that I in any way blame Mr Farraday, who is in no sense an unkind person; he was, I am sure, merely enjoying the sort of bantering which in the United States, no doubt, is a sign of a good, friendly understanding between employer and employee, indulged in as a kind of affectionate sport. Indeed, to put things into a proper perspective, I should point out that just such bantering on my new employer's part has characterized much of our relationship over these months – though I must confess, I remain rather unsure as to how I should respond.

Stevens employs characteristically formal language in this passage, with words such as 'propensity' and 'resident in'; it shows his strong connection with the past, his careful and precise nature and pedantic attention to 'correctness'. Furthermore, he reiterates to the reader his 'professional motive' for wanting to visit Miss Kenton and this raises the issue of the reader's perspective. On first reading, the reader has no other information to go on at this point in the **narrative**. However, after Stevens's meeting with Miss Kenton in Cornwall, the reader's perspective changes significantly – it becomes clear that Stevens loves Miss Kenton and she loves him. On reflection, all his protestations in this passage are untrue; he was telling *himself*, as much as the reader, that he had professional motives, in order to convince himself of this and to deny his true feelings. However, the extent of his protesting is perhaps a clue in itself: the reader may feel that he protests too much; and the more he denies something, the more he seems to be running and hiding from the truth.

In connection with Stevens's awareness of possible criticism, he also puts himself down and proclaims the errors he keeps making, from the faulty staff plan to his mistake in raising the subject of Miss Kenton at this time. Again, this excess of humility is in keeping with his job and also his lack of identity, but, as he says at the end of the novel, when he is facing the reality that is his life: 'whatever I do I find I am far from reaching the standards I once set myself. More and more errors are appearing in my work ... and I know what they signify ... I've given what I had to give. I gave it all to Lord Darlington' (p. 255). At the time of this extract, however, Stevens has not yet embarked upon his **literal** and **metaphorical** journey or begun to face what he is denying and trying to hide from, but he is at least aware of these errors.

When Farraday embarrasses him, Stevens draws a distinction between Farraday's behaviour and that of Lord Darlington. However, later in the novel this proves to be an example of Stevens's selective memory, that of a **narrator** who contradicts himself and does not realise he has done so. He says that Lord Darlington would never have placed an employee in such an embarrassing position, yet, at this time, he forgets – or chooses not to mention – that Lord Darlington once asked him to explain the facts of life to Reginald Cardinal. It is a humorous event for the reader when it is recounted later, although Stevens is unaware of the fact, just as he is unaware of the comedy of the situation here, especially when he stands awkwardly in front of the grinning Mr Farraday. A second, less humorous, example which Stevens mentions only later is when Lord Darlington calls for him one night and he is asked questions on political matters by Mr Spencer, questions that Stevens declines to answer. The failure to mention either of these examples here serves to show how carefully Stevens selects information and chooses to remember only certain facts about Lord Darlington, although at times the truth is inadvertently allowed to come to light.

In contrasting Mr Farraday and Lord Darlington here, Stevens highlights the cultural differences between the two men. He refers to the fact that Mr Farraday is an 'American gentleman' and his ways are different. This implicitly emphasises the 'Englishness' of Stevens and Lord Darlington, and feeds into the ideas about cultural identity which surface later on, particularly at the conference at Darlington Hall in 1923.

When Mr Farraday embarrasses Stevens, Stevens 'naturally' feels the 'temptation to deny immediately and unambiguously such motivations'. He justifies why he denies and represses these feelings – this is typical of his behaviour as a butler, and a sign of his excessive pursuit of his goal: to be a perfect butler like the one in his father's tale of the 'tiger under the table'. He takes this repression of feelings, as cited here, to a far greater level, however – for example, when his father dies during the conference and he keeps working, never faltering at his post.

Finally, this passage returns to the subject of bantering and Stevens admits: 'I remain rather unsure as to how I should respond.' This links in with the ending of the novel, when Stevens resolves 'to look at this whole matter of bantering more enthusiastically' (p. 258). By then he will have faced and admitted how empty and wasted his own life has been and realised that he has nothing to look forward to, unlike Miss Kenton, who has a husband, daughter and future grandchild to appreciate. In order to change, Stevens will have to realise that bantering is a way of reaching out to others and that it is people, not empty dreams, which must fill the void and give him a future to look forward to.

TEXT 2   (PAGES 157–8)

Coming at the end of the Moscombe chapter, the contrast in these juxtaposed responses to the dismissal of the Jewish maids is marked and typical of the relationship between Stevens and Miss Kenton. Stevens's persona is talking here and Miss Kenton openly shows her emotions. She questions Lord Darlington's judgement and suggests that his actions constitute a wrong of biblical proportions with the word 'sin'. Stevens clearly demonstrates 'the mindless sort of "loyalty"' he is contemptuous of later (p. 210). His worship of Lord Darlington and trust in him extends this far. The reader can see that this is anything but a trivial and insignificant event, as Stevens has described it when defending Lord Darlington, and that he is not as morally good as Stevens has portrayed him. It is **ironic** that Stevens describes the world outside as being 'treacherous', when there is treachery within Darlington Hall itself, and furthermore, that Stevens has become the tool for enforcing it in this particular case.

> 'Mr Stevens, I am outraged that you can sit there and utter what you have just done as though you were discussing orders for the larder. I simply cannot believe it. You are saying Ruth and Sarah are to be dismissed on the grounds that they are Jewish?'

> 'Miss Kenton, I have just this moment explained the situation to you fully. His lordship has made his decision and there is nothing for you and me to debate over.'

> 'Does it not occur to you, Mr Stevens, that to dismiss Ruth and Sarah on these grounds would be simply – *wrong*? I will not stand for such things. I will not work in a house in which such things can occur.'

> 'Miss Kenton, I will ask you not to excite yourself and to conduct yourself in a manner befitting your position. This is a very straightforward matter. If his lordship wishes these particular contracts to be discontinued, then there is little more to be said.'

> 'I am warning you, Mr Stevens, I will not continue to work in such a house. If my girls are dismissed, I will leave also.'

> 'Miss Kenton, I am surprised to find you reacting in this manner. Surely I don't have to remind you that our professional duty is not to our own foibles and sentiments, but to the wishes of our employer.'

> 'I am telling you, Mr Stevens, if you dismiss my girls tomorrow, it will be wrong, a sin as any sin ever was one and I will not continue to work in such a house.'

'Miss Kenton, let me suggest to you that you are hardly well placed to be passing judgements of such a high and mighty nature. The fact is, the world of today is a very complicated and treacherous place. There are many things you and I are simply not in a position to understand concerning, say, the nature of Jewry. Whereas his lordship, I might venture, is somewhat better placed to judge what is for the best. Now, Miss Kenton, I really must retire. I thank you again for the cocoa. Ten thirty tomorrow morning. Send the two employees concerned, please.'

It was evident from the moment the two maids stepped into my pantry the following morning that Miss Kenton had already spoken to them, for they both came in sobbing. I explained the situation to them as briefly as possible, underlining that their work had been satisfactory and that they would, accordingly, receive good references. As I recall, neither of them said anything of note throughout the whole interview, which lasted perhaps three or four minutes, and they left sobbing just as they had arrived.

Miss Kenton's outrage is natural and right, yet one cannot help also agreeing to some extent with Stevens, in that neither he nor Miss Kenton are in a strong enough position to stop the dismissal from happening. What is unforgivable, however, is allowing it to happen with no protest and no reaction but indifference.

The maids are real people to Miss Kenton. She calls them 'my girls', a sign of her personal interest in them, and also by their first names, Ruth and Sarah, a personal, human touch which contrasts with the attitude of Stevens (whose first name we never learn). Stevens refers to 'these particular contracts' and 'the two employees', an indication of distance and dehumanisation. It is his way of maintaining his persona, the smooth exterior, and keeping his own feelings at bay. He certainly betrays no emotion here and seems almost inhuman in his manner and attitude. Hence the reader, like Miss Kenton, is surprised to learn that he was 'distressed' by what he comes to call a 'misunderstanding' (p. 161) in the summerhouse about a year later.

Here, Stevens describes the actual dismissal of the maids in a few short lines, perhaps a sign of his hidden and repressed guilt and revulsion about the incident. Elsewhere, he spends over three times the number of lines discussing silver polish (pp. 141–3) and how it contributed to Lord Darlington's political aims, and he spends a long paragraph describing the banqueting hall at the conference of 1923 (p. 102). These passages clearly show how Stevens is more at home in the world of objects and surfaces. Emotions, uncomfortable situations and anger are threatening to him: he merely wants to do his duty and that is what he hides behind in the case of the Jewish maids' dismissal.

Stevens addresses Miss Kenton as 'you and I' in this passage. He often refers to the implied reader as 'the likes of you and I' and he speaks similarly here in an echo of this. It is comparable with the way he addresses his father in the third person and it becomes a possible clue as to who the 'you' in the novel might be intended to refer to.

TEXT 3   (PAGES 251–2)

This tender exchange from the final chapter of the novel is filled with **pathos** and changes the reader's perspective on Stevens and Miss Kenton's relationship completely. It causes the reader to reflect back over their encounters and see them as they truly are: they are not only 'professional', as Stevens persistently claims.

'I feel I should answer you, Mr Stevens. As you say, we may not meet again for many years. Yes, I do love my husband. I didn't at first. I didn't at first for a long time. When I left Darlington Hall all those years ago, I never realized I was really, truly leaving. I believe I thought of it as simply another ruse, Mr Stevens, to annoy you. It was a shock to come out here and find myself married. For a long time, I was very unhappy, very unhappy indeed. But then year after year went by, there was the war, Catherine grew up, and one day I realized I loved my husband. You spend so much time with someone, you find you get used to him. He's a kind, steady man, and yes, Mr Stevens, I've grown to love him.'

Miss Kenton fell silent again for a moment. Then she went on:

'But that doesn't mean to say, of course, there aren't occasions now and then – extremely desolate occasions – when you think to yourself: "What a terrible mistake I've made with my life." And you get to thinking about a different life, a *better* life you might have had. For instance, I get to thinking about a life I might have had with you, Mr Stevens. And I suppose that's when I get angry over some trivial little thing and leave. But each time I do so, I realize before long – my rightful place is with my husband. After all, there's no turning back the clock now. One can't be forever dwelling on what might have been. One should realize one has as good as most, perhaps better, and be grateful.'

I do not think I responded immediately, for it took me a moment or two to fully digest these words of Miss Kenton. Moreover, as you might appreciate, their implications were such as to provoke a certain degree of sorrow within me. Indeed – why should I not admit it? – at that moment, my heart was breaking. Before long, however, I turned to her and said with a smile:

'You're very correct, Mrs Benn. As you say, it is too late to turn back the clock. Indeed, I would not be able to rest if I thought such ideas were the cause of unhappiness for you and your husband. We must each of us, as you point out, be grateful for what we *do* have.'

The typical politeness and restraint of this exchange serve to heighten its tragedy. Miss Kenton's confession of dreaming of a life with Stevens is as near to a declaration of love as she will ever give and mirrors his own mention of having 'dreams' (p. 189). In a moment of **dramatic irony**, Stevens admits to the reader, but not to Miss Kenton, that his heart was broken by her words and this, equally, is as near a declaration of love for her as he can give. It is also the realisation of exactly what he has sacrificed for Lord Darlington, who ultimately was not worth it, and this is the start of Stevens's process of facing up to the monumental waste his life has been. Stevens, whose persona has prevailed over the death of his father and Miss Kenton's marriage to Mr Benn, has a heart, emotions and passions after all, yet he remains weak. He cannot look at her until the bus arrives and he sees her tears.

Typically, she has the emotional strength and courage to declare her feelings. Their conversation here echoes their past exchanges – again he gives her no encouragement, and instead hides his heartbreak with a smile, the device he employs to mask pain, and lets her go, kindly. It is no wonder that she devised 'ruses' to annoy Stevens during her time at the Hall, in order to try to provoke a response from him, to get to know him, to see behind his persona. It seems in this passage that she never lost her belief in him, and her whole being centred around him, and this is why she was in shock to find herself married to Mr Benn, as though she had been in a dream. She had wanted marriage and a baby and thought they would fulfil her, but **ironically**, they did not; she was unhappy, and kept trying to escape by leaving for a few days. It was Stevens who could have made her happy, but chose not to. There is further irony in that she returns to her husband out of a sense of duty – duty being Stevens's motivation for rejecting her in the first place. Furthermore, it is 'trivial' events that trigger her leaving in the first place. In this respect she mirrors Stevens as for her, too, trivial events signify greater things (see Themes).

Finally, the advice Miss Kenton gives Stevens, about being unable to turn back the clock and being grateful for what one has, is a prophecy of the advice he will receive from the retired butler on the pier at Weymouth. She clearly feels a similar sense of waste to that of Stevens, but has the wisdom to focus instead on the positive and to value her 'kind, steady' husband, to cherish her daughter and look forward to the arrival of her grandchild. Stevens agrees with her on this issue, but is in no position to accept the advice at this time, since he is facing the loss of her and her love and is almost overwhelmed by emotion – which still he manages to hide. Ishiguro makes use of **pathetic fallacy** as they are sitting in 'drizzle' (p. 250) during the conversation, and the overall tone of the exchange is one of dignity, something Stevens actually attains here, but cannot see.

PART FIVE

BACKGROUND

KAZUO ISHIGURO

Kazuo Ishiguro was born in Nagasaki, Japan, in 1954 and came to England when he was five years old. He lived in Scotland and was a grouse-beater at Balmoral Castle, Aberdeen. He later worked as a community worker in Renfrew, Scotland, and as a residential social worker in London. He went to the University of Kent at Canterbury and gained a BA with honours in English and Philosophy in 1978. In 1980 he received a Creative Writing MA from the University of East Anglia. His first novel, *A Pale View of Hills*, was published in 1982. Kazuo Ishiguro is married with a daughter and lives in London.

A Pale View of Hills won the Winifred Holtby Prize and was followed by *An Artist of the Floating World* in 1986. This second novel won the Whitbread Book of the Year Award and was shortlisted for the Booker Prize. Ishiguro won the Booker Prize in 1989 for *The Remains of the Day*. It was made into a successful film by Merchant–Ivory in 1993, starring Anthony Hopkins, Emma Thompson and Christopher Reeve. Kazuo Ishiguro's fourth novel, *The Unconsoled*, was published in 1995. He has also written two original screenplays for Channel Four, *A Profile of J. Arthur Mason* and *The Gourmet*.

HISTORICAL BACKGROUND

There are two main historical areas which form a backdrop to the events in *The Remains of the Day*. The first is the Suez Crisis of 1956, when the novel opens. The United States and Britain had previously agreed to finance the Aswan High Dam, an engineering project on the Nile river in southern Egypt, but they withdrew this offer because of the growing ties between Egypt and the Soviet Union. President Nasser of Egypt reacted to the withdrawal of funding for the Dam by seizing control of the Suez Canal Company on 26 July 1956 and imposing tolls upon vessels using the Canal, to pay for the construction costs of the

Dam. As the Canal is the easiest, most convenient and thus cheapest route for shipping petroleum from the Persian Gulf to Europe, this had serious ramifications for European leaders, who depended upon these shipments. The UK and France were concerned that Nasser might close the Canal altogether. Diplomatic efforts to settle the crisis failed and Britain, France and Israel plotted military action, which began in October 1956, but was opposed by the United Nations and the Soviet Union. By November 1956, a truce was arranged and the military action ceased. Nasser was victorious; the UK and France lost their influence in the Middle East as a consequence.

These events would have been dominating England at the time Stevens was writing (the Prologue is dated as July 1956), yet Stevens makes no reference to them whatsoever. The significance of this is that he is still so focused on his vision of being a perfect butler that he is oblivious to all events which have no direct influence over him. In 1936, he says to Reginald Cardinal that he has 'failed to notice any such development' (p. 233). Here, Reginald Cardinal has been referring to the rise of the Nazis and Adolf Hitler. To a modern reader, it seems beyond belief that any person living in England during the 1930s could not notice Hitler and the Nazis, but it is testament to Stevens's concentration on his goal and his staggering devotion to his vision. Having failed to be aware of Adolf Hitler in 1936, it is not surprising that he is oblivious of the Suez Crisis in 1956.

The second area of historical focus is the rise of fascism during the 1920s and 1930s in Germany and, to some extent, England. When Germany lost the First World War, many Germans looked for someone to blame, a scapegoat for their humiliating defeat. Rumours began to circulate that Germany signed the Treaty of Versailles because they had been betrayed by Bolsheviks and Jews. These rumours grew and soon Jews were being blamed for all Germany's problems. There were more Jews in Germany than Bolsheviks and so the Jews were more of a 'visible' target as scapegoats. The Treaty of Versailles caused hardship to Germany and the German people. The economy collapsed, unemployment rose, reparation payments had to be made and people were starving to death. There were endless cries for a strong leader and many political groups sprang up, including the National Socialist German Workers' Party (the Nazi Party). They were opposed to democracy and liberalism, and (despite the use of the word 'Socialist' in their name) were fascists. The Austrian-born Adolf Hitler (1889–1945) went to work full-time for this party in April 1920, after serving in the Bavarian Army during the First World War. In 1921, he became Chairman of the party; at this stage they were a small, but radical, group dedicated to old-fashioned values, patriotism and anti-Semitism (anti-Jewishness). The German people turned to them increasingly because of these beliefs and their power slowly grew. The party also ensured the growth of their power by using violent methods, such as intimidation, robbery, attacks, incitement to revolution, even murder. Members of their paramilitary wing were known as the Brownshirts or the Stormtroopers.

Despite their increasing success during the 1920s, they were not elected to the government in the 1928 elections, but the Great Depression of the 1930s, following the Wall Street Crash in 1929, helped the party grow from strength to strength as Germany's plight became even more desperate. The world was suffering from an economic slump and Germany, already in chaos, was the hardest hit. By 1932, there were thirty different political parties in Germany, all offering salvation to the people. Both Nazism and Marxism rose at this time and became the two main parties. The Marxists wanted a Germany modelled on the Soviet Union and were against the ruling classes, whereas the Nazi message was that the Treaty of Versailles was a crime, the Jews were to blame, Marxism had to be stamped out and Germany would be reborn.

The Nazis offered order, discipline and Hitler's personality – he was a strong man to rescue Germany – but not much in terms of policies. In the election of 1932, Hitler was seen as a credible possibility as leader, but he lost to President Hindenburg. Hitler became Chancellor in January 1933 and gained dictatorial powers on 25 March 1933. Hindenburg was thus only a figurehead. When Hindenburg died in 1934, Hitler became overall ruler of Germany.

When Hitler became Chancellor, his first targets were his political opponents, the Marxists. They were thrown into concentration camps, along with other anti-Nazis. A reign of terror began. Hitler had great visions for Germany, and his top priority was rearmament, which was prohibited by the Treaty of Versailles. In 1935, Germany began openly rearming. Hitler sent troops into the Rhineland and annexed the

Sudetenland (in Czechoslovakia) in 1938. Despite these violations of the Treaty of Versailles, the rest of Europe, including Britain, did nothing to stop Hitler. His power and Germany's confidence grew. It was his invasion of Poland that finally roused the Allies to try to stop him, and war was declared in September 1939.

While Hitler was gaining power in Germany, fascism became popular briefly in England amongst a small group of people led by Sir Oswald Mosley (1896–1980). Having served in the Royal Flying Corps during the First World War, he entered the House of Commons in 1918 and served as a Conservative, an Independent and as a member of the Labour Party. In 1931, he left, and after a visit to Italy he founded the British Union of Fascists in 1932. Also known as the 'blackshirts', they supported Hitler (who was a guest at Mosley's wedding) and incited violence in Jewish areas of East London. Mosley was imprisoned by the British Government between 1940 and 1943. Upon release, he tried to start his Union up again, but failed.

Literary background

The motoring trip that Stevens undertakes, and his descriptions of places en route, could lead to the novel being categorised as fictional 'travel writing'. However, the motoring trip is also a **metaphor** for Stevens's psychological journey (see Imagery & Symbolism), a way of framing the novel and the excuse for Stevens to go to visit Miss Kenton. In fact, *The Remains of the Day* is really no more 'travel writing' of the fictional kind than Evelyn Waugh's *Black Mischief* is. Waugh's novel, set in the fictional country of Azania, focuses primarily on upper-class Englishman Basil Seal, who travels to Azania and has various adventures, but his journey is largely a backdrop for Waugh's biting **satire**. Similarly in *The Remains of the Day*, there are some details about places such as Salisbury, but they are incidental and subservient to the **flashbacks** of Stevens's memory. The places have a greater role in triggering thoughts and reflections, such as the view that the old man directs Stevens to in the Salisbury chapter.

The novel is closer to a fictive autobiography, like, for example, Charlotte Brontë's *Jane Eyre* and Anne Brontë's *Agnes Grey*. These are two novels which tell the story of the narrator's life in the first person, with no corroborating evidence; like *The Remains of the Day*, they focus on carefully selected moments in time. However, *The Remains of the Day*, unlike *Jane Eyre* and *Agnes Grey*, gives little or no detail about the narrator's childhood with his family, which might be expected from more conventional fictive autobiography. Indeed, Stevens's mother is never mentioned, while his brother, Leonard, is only mentioned in connection with the tale about the General. Yet the novel is revealing and confessional. It is unlike typical autobiographies as it includes an ongoing debate about what makes a 'great' butler and dignity, and its chronology is unconventionally ordered, combining a present-day account of a journey in a car with flashbacks to the past.

The narrative is very personal and, as such, Ishiguro has written Stevens's account of events in a way that is personal to him, lending the tale an authenticity, as memories are provoked and unfold so that something new about Stevens can be learned. In this way, the novel defies categorising. A study of Ishiguro's other works is revealing, as there are themes and preoccupations which resonate throughout his texts. Brian Shaffer explores Ishiguro's style in the opening chapter to *Understanding Kazuo Ishiguro* (see Further Reading), stating that Ishiguro 'is more a novelist of the inner character than of the outer world ... What preoccupies the novelist is psychological defences and the "emotional arena" most broadly construed: the suppression of emotion' (p. 8). Shaffer detects literary influences upon Ishiguro that include E.M. Forster, Ford Madox Ford, Henry James and Franz Kafka. Perhaps, ultimately, it is more useful to focus on *The Remains of the Day* as a study of Stevens's psyche and as an unfolding of a tightly closed human heart, rather than searching for categories and definitions into which the novel fits. Its uniqueness rests in the very fact that Stevens is a unique, albeit obsessed and troubled, individual and the novel is, whilst fictive, his own.

PART SIX

CRITICAL HISTORY & BROADER PERSPECTIVES

CRITICAL RECEPTION

The book jacket for the 1993 Faber and Faber film tie-in edition of *The Remains of the Day* cites a number of critical reactions to the novel which appeared in the media, for example: 'Almost unbearably moving' (*The Listener*) and '*The Remains of the Day* is a triumph ... This wholly convincing portrait of a human life unweaving before your eyes is inventive and absorbing, by turns funny, absurd, and ultimately very moving' (*The Sunday Times*). It is clear that the novel's reception has been favourable – it won the Booker Prize and was made into an Oscar-winning film. What is surprising, then, to a present-day scholar of this contemporary novel, is that there have been so few critical works published in Britain about Kazuo Ishiguro. Contemporary literary criticism in general appears to have overlooked *The Remains of the Day*. It has by no means been explored to its fullest extent, and only small headway has been made by critics, even those taking a **psychoanalytical** stance, to which the novel seems well suited. For example, Brian Shaffer's bibliography (see Further Reading) cites twenty-three book reviews, ten articles, and ten interviews and profiles – and this covers all of Ishiguro's work, not just *The Remains of the Day*. Perhaps the highest verbal praise comes from Stanley Kauffmann, who wrote: 'About *The Remains of the Day* it is possible to risk the word "perfect"' ('The Floating World', *The New Republic*, 6 November 1995, p. 43). Despite the dearth of material on Kazuo Ishiguro and his works to date, however, it is worth considering the novel from a critical point of view and forming one's own opinion.

CRITICAL STANDPOINTS

A **Structuralist** approach to the novel would provide an interesting insight into the way Stevens narrates his story. Structuralism presents the theory that the relationship between words themselves and what they actually mean is arbitrary, i.e. the word 'pen' and an actual pen do not necessarily bear any relation to each other. When we look at Stevens's narrative we soon realise that what he says is unreliable, the literal meaning is not necessarily what we see as the 'real' meaning, and this unreliability points towards a 'slippage' between what is written and what is meant.

Post-Structuralism also provides a useful insight into the novel. This school of thought concentrates on the way meaning is produced when we read. One of the main arguments of Post-Structuralism is that once a text has been read, and a reader has placed his or her own interpretation of its meaning on to it, the meaning that the author originally 'wrote' becomes obsolete. This theory was expounded by Roland Barthes in his essay 'The Death of the Author'. Here he states that 'The birth of the reader must be at the cost of the death of the author'. He also draws a distinction between texts where the reader is passive, and texts where the reader needs to take an active role in order to elucidate meaning. Post-Structuralists would argue that by reading Stevens's narrative, the reader 'reads' a different meaning from what Stevens has written. The fact that Stevens is an unreliable narrator positively invites the reader to make their own meaning, and as the reader is 'born', the author (in this case the narrator) 'dies' - we come to trust our own 'reading' more than what Stevens literally tells us in his narrative. This way of looking at *The Remains of the Day* is complicated, however, by the fact that Stevens is not the author, he is the narrator 'written' by the author. Within the novel itself Stevens is the 'author' and he writes for an implied reader, who, we can assume, is a fellow servant (see Narrative Techniques). However, standing outside the frame of the novel are Ishiguro, the real author, and the real reader. It is only Ishiguro and the real reader who can fully see the 'true' meaning of the novel.

Marxist criticism might focus upon Stevens as an oppressed worker, trapped by the upper class, in the form of Lord Darlington, his employer, and enslaved by the class system and a lack of money. It is important, however, not to ignore Stevens's own compliance with his role and position, a compliance that is motivated by his desire to emulate his father and worship Lord Darlington. He does not seem to be suffering from internalised oppression – rather, he is guided by his obsessive vision of being the perfect butler serving the perfect man. This vision is grounded in his psychological makeup rather than Lord Darlington's feudal beliefs. Stevens does acknowledge the limits of his position, though, at the end of the Moscombe chapter and he does have a point: in the context of the class system and rigid social hierarchy, it was not his place to comment on his employer or involve himself in his affairs.

A **feminist** perspective might focus upon Miss Kenton as an oppressed female in a patriarchal society, forced to choose between her job and marriage. Bearing in mind that part of the tragedy of the story is her part in the unrealised love relationship, she is characterised by needing a man, marriage and a baby in order to find fulfilment, and thus seems to be stereotypically portrayed. Certainly, the women in the novel are apparently stereotypical as they are generally presented as scheming (Carolyn Barnet), oppressed (Ruth and Sarah) or foolish (Lisa). Yet Ishiguro twists the portrayal of Miss Kenton by exploding the stereotype he has set up, to show that she is not fulfilled by marriage after all: it is Stevens with whom she believes she will find fulfilment, and we learn at the end that she had all she thought she wanted with Mr Benn, but was still unfulfilled because she was not with Stevens, the man she loves. Within this patriarchal society, Miss Kenton is a strong-minded woman who speaks her mind and shows her feelings, usually anger towards Stevens. She questions Lord Darlington's actions over the sacking of the Jewish maids, but lacks the courage to leave the Hall as she threatens to, although she reveals it is because she does not want to leave Stevens. Ultimately, feminist critics might argue that she remains oppressed by society in general and by Stevens in particular; she is even denied her own voice in the novel and Stevens speaks for her, as he is the sole **narrator** and all events are interpreted and retold by him.

The Remains of the Day might well become a popular text with **psychoanalytic** critics who grapple with Stevens's mental journey and the fact that he is the sole **narrator**. Stevens certainly could be studied as a 'case' for psychoanalysis and much of the content and form of the novel inherently provoke this kind of reading. The triangular relationship between Stevens, Lord Darlington and Stevens's father could be read from Freudian or Lacanian perspectives, to provide further insights into Stevens's identity suppression and his need for a persona.

A student of *The Remains of the Day* may find it very useful to read any of Kazuo Ishiguro's other works, to gain insights into content, characterisation, themes and written style. His other novels are: *A Pale View of Hills* (1982), *An Artist of the Floating World* (1986) and *The Unconsoled* (1995). Yet to be published by Faber and Faber is his forthcoming novel, *When We Were Orphans*.

In terms of works about Ishiguro's novels, the best place to start is *Understanding Kazuo Ishiguro* by Brian W. Shaffer (University of South Carolina Press, 1998). To date, it is the only book about Ishiguro that has been published in Britain, and its bibliography provides pointers to forty-three articles, interviews and so forth. The opening chapter contains information about Ishiguro, his influences and his written style, and the subsequent four chapters focus on Ishiguro's four published novels, including *The Remains of the Day*. Some interesting detail and insight on the novel is provided, but Shaffer's book is most useful for gaining a general overview of Ishiguro's work and his central themes and ideas.

In the USA, *Narratives of Memory and Identity: The Novels of Kazuo Ishiguro* (Mike Petry, *Aachen British and American Studies* volume 12, October 1999) has been published in hardback by Peter Lang Publishing, but has yet to appear in Britain. In addition, an Internet search for articles on Ishiguro's works can be rewarding, although the quality of writing varies considerably.

The 1993 Merchant–Ivory film of *The Remains of the Day*, directed by James Ivory, stars Anthony Hopkins (as Stevens) and Emma Thompson (as Miss Kenton). It was filmed in Devon, at Powderham Castle (near the interestingly named town of Kenton) and Exeter. (The castle is open to the public in spring and summer and could form part of a motoring tour like the one Stevens took.)

There are a great number of historical and sociological books on fascism and class. It is perhaps more rewarding to adopt a literary approach for insights and understanding about the concepts and themes explored in *The Remains of the Day* – the works below are suggested possibilities for such an approach.

Jane Austen, *Sense and Sensibility* (1811) and *Emma* (1816)

These novels focus in a satirical way on class issues and snobbery in the nineteenth century, while providing insights into 'gentlemanly' behaviour through the characters of Mr Knightly (in *Emma*) and Colonel Brandon (in *Sense and Sensibility*), of whom Lord Darlington is reminiscent

John Betjeman, *Collected Poems* (1958) and *The Best of* (ed. Guest, 1978)
The former poet laureate's often humorous work focuses on characteristics of England, especially in the 1930s–1950s period

Bertolt Brecht, *Mother Courage and Her Children* (1941)
This play provides a fascinating look at the tragedy of war and totalitarian rule

Anne Brontë, *Agnes Grey* (1847) and Charlotte Brontë, *Jane Eyre* (1847)
These novels, by two of the Brontë sisters, both depict attitudes to servants as second-class citizens and reveal insights into the life of a servant from the servant's own point of view

E.M. Forster, *Where Angels Fear to Tread* (1905), *A Room with a View* (1908) and *Howard's End* (1910)
Three novels which are indispensable for a grasp of the Edwardian values and 'Englishness' which resonated into the 1920s and 1930s; they also provide vivid slices of society's attitudes to class and status

Aldous Huxley, *Brave New World* (1932)
Often compared to Orwell's *Nineteen Eighty-four*, this novel depicts a future England in which the state's power over the individual is total; many aspects of Huxley's fictional society seem prophetic in the light of Hitler's subsequent rise to power (see Historical Background)

Christopher Isherwood, *Goodbye to Berlin* (1939)
A portrayal of the decadence in 1930s Germany leading to the rise of Hitler. The novel was translated to the cinema as the Oscar-winning film *Cabaret* (1972), directed by Bob Fosse

George Orwell, *Down and Out in London and Paris* (1933), *Nineteen Eighty-four* (1949), *Animal Farm* (1945) and *Collected Essays, Journalism and Letters* (1968)
In his novels and his non-fictional work, George Orwell was continually interested by class attitudes, and how a state/government might act in order to protect itself and ensure the growth of its power

D.H. Lawrence, *Sons and Lovers* (1913) and *The Rainbow* (1915)
These novels portray rural English working-class life and the 'ordinary' person (as opposed to the upper classes), such as Stevens encounters on his drive to Cornwall

Jessica Mitford, *Hons and Rebels* (1960)

> This is a fascinating look at the childhood of aristocrat Jessica Mitford's sisters
> Unity, who was a friend of Adolf Hitler, and Diana, who married Oswald Mosley
> (see Historical Background)

Nancy Mitford, *Love in a Cold Climate* (1976)

> An upper-class love story, written by the oldest of the Mitford sisters, which
> explores attitudes in 1930s England

J.B. Priestley, *An Inspector Calls* (1945)

> A play which touches on issues of class and snobbery

Erich Maria Remarque, *All Quiet on the Western Front* (1929)

> A novel detailing experiences of the First World War from a German point
> of view

Siegfried Sassoon, *Memoirs of a Fox-hunting Man* (1928), *Memoirs of an Infantry Officer* (1930) and *Collected Poetry* (1961)

> Sassoon's poetry and prose work captures upper-class life, such as Lord Darlington
> might have experienced, as well as giving insights into the suffering of the First
> World War

George Bernard Shaw, *Pygmalion* (1912)

> This play reveals class attitudes, but is also interesting for the creation of Eliza
> Doolittle's 'persona', which Stevens's self-constructed persona echoes

Evelyn Waugh, *Black Mischief* (1932), *A Handful of Dust* (1934), *Put Out More Flags* (1942) and *Brideshead Revisited* (1945)

> Waugh's satirical novels focus on upper-class life, particularly in the 1930s, and
> reveal upper-class attitudes and facets of pre-Second World War England and
> Englishness. Of particular interest, as they both link to Lord Darlington and
> Darlington Hall, are *A Handful of Dust*, which focuses on the great house Hetton
> Abbey and its owner, Tony Last, and *Brideshead Revisited*, in which Charles Ryder
> presents Brideshead and the Flyte family from the point of view of an outsider
> looking in on their world.

	World events	Events in the novel
1851		Stevens's father William is born
1859-69	Construction of the Suez Canal	
1880-1	The first of two wars fought between the British and the Boers for control of South Africa ends with the defeat of the British at Majuba Hill	
1899-1902	The second Boer War in South Africa leads to the Peace of Vereeniging; in Britain, Edward VII accedes to the throne following the death of Queen Victoria in 1901	Stevens is a boy when his elder brother, Leonard, is killed during the war; whilst a boy, Stevens often hears his father recount a story about a tiger under a table in India
1910	Edward VII is succeeded by George V, who renames the royal line the House of Windsor, thereby breaking ties with their German ancestry	
1912		Stevens's father acts as a valet to 'the General'; he is at the height of his career, working for the industrialist Mr John Silvers; he works for Mr Silvers for fifteen years, during which time he chastises some drunken gentlemen; around this time, Stevens starts out as a footman under his father's supervision and later gains his first post as butler to Mr and Mrs Muggeridge in Oxfordshire
1914-18	The First World War claims more than 8 million lives; in 1917, revolution breaks out in Russia	
1918		Stevens begins working at Darlington Hall
1918-20		Herr Bremann visits Darlington Hall and becomes close friends with Lord Darlington
1919	The Treaty of Versailles is signed at the Paris Peace Conference, imposing reparation payments on Germany and ensuring the demilitarisation of the Rhineland	
1920		Towards the end of the year, Lord Darlington makes the first of a number of trips to Berlin
1920-22		One winter's night, Lord Darlington discusses the Treaty of Versailles with Sir Richard Fox; some time later, Herr Bremann shoots himself and in the following weeks Lord Darlington spends more and more time on the crisis in Germany and prominent political and social figures visit the house; Sir David Cardinal becomes a close friend and ally of Lord Darlington

World events	Events in the novel

1922 — Benito Mussolini assumes dictatorial powers in Italy — In the spring, Stevens's father and Miss Kenton come to work at Darlington Hall; Lord Darlington tries to gather prominent figures at his house before the great conference in Italy in the spring, in order to ensure a 'satisfactory outcome'; the gathering at Darlington Hall is unable to take place, due to insufficient time, but since the conference in Italy ends in indecision, Lord Darlington plans to hold a gathering before the next great conference, due to take place in Switzerland the following year

1923 — With other right-wing extremists, Adolf Hitler attempts to overthrow the government of Bavaria — In the last week of March, the planned conference at Darlington Hall takes place; Stevens's father has had a fall a couple of weeks prior to this and becomes ill as the conference begins; he remains seriously ill as the conference progresses and dies during the second and final dinner of the conference, where the American politician Mr Lewis calls Lord Darlington an 'amateur'

1929 — The Wall Street Crash precipitates the Great Depression; high levels of unemployment and a slump in prices and industrial output continue worldwide throughout the 1930s

1931 — Formation of the British Commonwealth of Nations

1932 — Oswald Mosley founds the British Union of Fascists; his 'blackshirts' support Hitler and incite anti-Semitic violence — During the summer, Carolyn Barnet, a member of the 'blackshirts', is a regular visitor at Darlington Hall; Lord Darlington dismisses two maids because they are Jewish; Lisa joins the staff but eight or nine months later elopes with the second footman; Miss Kenton and Stevens fall out over the incident with the Jewish maids – she disagrees with it and he accepts it because Lord Darlington wishes it – and Miss Kenton has 'pride before a fall' in her faith in Lisa

1933 — Adolf Hitler is appointed Chancellor of Germany at President Hindenburg's request; the persecution of Jews becomes increasingly systematic — Lord Darlington has severed his connection with the blackshirts and Mrs Barnet; he expresses his regret at his decision to fire the Jewish maids; around this time Sir David Cardinal is killed in a riding accident; the Hayes Society, which has been a powerful club for butlers of the first rank during the 1920s and 1930s, is forced to close

World events	Events in the novel
1935 Stanley Baldwin is elected British Prime Minister; Anthony Eden is appointed Foreign Secretary; Mussolini invades Abyssinia; the Nazis' Nuremberg Laws formalise discrimination against German Jews and other 'non-Aryans'	One night Lord Darlington summons Stevens so that his guest, Mr Spencer, can ask for Stevens's opinion on various political matters, which Stevens declines to give; the next day, as he is apologising, Lord Darlington reveals his firm belief in fascism, saying that democracy is outmoded, and he praises the strong leadership in Italy and Germany
1936 Edward VIII succeeds George V as King, but abdicates later in the year in order to marry Wallis Simpson; his brother succeeds him as George VI; Hitler occupies the Rhineland, in violation of the Treaty of Versailles; after achieving victory in Abyssinia, Mussolini agrees to an alliance with Hitler known as the Rome–Berlin Axis	Stevens's relationship with Miss Kenton changes; she catches him reading a romantic novel and there is a change in atmosphere as she stands in front of him; Miss Kenton receives letters and takes time off; her aunt dies, and some months afterwards, Reginald Cardinal arrives at the house unexpectedly; Miss Kenton tells Stevens that she has had a proposal of marriage from Mr Benn, before going out for the evening; at around 8.40 pm Herr Ribbentrop, the German Ambassador, arrives at the house, although this is not his first visit; the British Prime Minister and Foreign Secretary are also present; Miss Kenton returns and tells Stevens she has accepted Mr Benn's proposal, then spitefully ridicules Stevens; Mr Cardinal tells Stevens of the danger of Lord Darlington's ties to Germany and how he is being manipulated by the Nazis; Stevens remains impartial and says that he has failed to notice the rise of Hitler and the Nazis; Miss Kenton leaves Darlington Hall to marry Mr Benn and move to Cornwall
1937 Neville Chamberlain succeeds Stanley Baldwin as Prime Minister	
1938 The Munich Agreement, signed by Chamberlain, Hitler, Mussolini and France's Edouard Daladier, allows Germany to regain possession of the Sudetenland; Anthony Eden resigns as Foreign Secretary over Chamberlain's dealings with Nazi Germany, but returns to government when war breaks out	

World events	Events in the novel
1939-45 Germany's invasion of Poland in September 1939 initiates the Second World War, during which more than 20 million lives are lost; an estimated 6 million Jews and 1 million others are killed in Nazi concentration camps; the conflict ends with the German surrender at Rheims and the Japanese surrender a few months later, following the USA's use of atomic bombs at Hiroshima and Nagasaki	During the war, Reginald Cardinal is killed in Belgium; a newspaper publishes articles about Lord Darlington and his Nazi connections; Miss Kenton has a child, Catherine, and slowly begins to love her husband
1946 War crimes trials conclude at Nuremberg, with Ribbentrop and others sentenced to death	Lord Darlington unsuccessfully sues the newspaper over its 'slanderous articles'; he has fallen from grace in society, and he becomes virtually an invalid
1949	Dr Carlisle moves to Moscombe, Devon, and is at this point a firm believer in socialism
1951 Winston Churchill returns as British Prime Minister	
1952 King George VI dies and is succeeded by Elizabeth II; a coup led by Gamel Abd al-Nasser and Mohammed Naguib overthrows the monarchy in Egypt	
1953 Egypt is declared a republic	Lord Darlington dies
1955 Following Winston Churchill's resignation, Anthony Eden becomes Prime Minister	Mr Farraday buys Darlington Hall, but does not move in for four months
1956 In June, Nasser is elected president of Egypt; the USA withdraws financial backing from the Aswan High Dam project in response to Egypt's dealings with the USSR; in July, the Suez Canal Company is nationalised by Nasser, to provide revenue for the dam project; after an attack by Israel in October, the UK and France propose temporary occupation, asking both sides to withdraw from the Canal Zone; Egypt's rejection of this plan leads to invasion by British and French forces, but diplomatic pressure from the USSR and the USA leads to their withdrawal and the resignation of Anthony Eden	In July, Stevens writes the Prologue; prior to this, Stevens has denied working for Lord Darlington when Mr Farraday has friends to visit; in August and September, for five weeks, Mr Farraday returns to the USA; two weeks before his return, Stevens borrows the Ford and drives to visit Miss Kenton in Cornwall; at the end of the novel Stevens is sitting on the pier in Weymouth during his return journey to Darlington Hall

anti-hero a character in a work of literature who is unheroic or a failure, particularly one who is unable to perform deeds of bravery or generosity

colloquialism the use of the kinds of expression and grammar associated with ordinary, everyday speech rather than formal language

diction a general term used to describe the kind of vocabulary used in a work of literature

dramatic irony a feature of a play whereby the development of the plot allows the audience more information about what is happening than some of the characters themselves have; the term can also be used to describe a similar situation in a novel

elegy specifically, a poem of lamentation, usually focusing on the death of a single person. More generally, the term 'elegy' can also be used to describe any work of literature which focuses on the passing of a person, era or cultural movement

empathy to empathise is to mentally identify with a character in a story, to the point of fully understanding his or her thoughts, feelings and actions

feminism a tenet of feminist thought is that male ways of perceiving and ordering are 'inscribed' into the prevailing ideology of society: women are subordinated because they are perceived through a constantly repeated framework of negative perceptions which are ingrained in language. Women are thus conditioned to enter society accepting their own inferiority, and even co-operating in and approving its perpetuation. Femininity is regarded as a construct of society. A task of feminist criticism, therefore, is to examine and re-evaluate literature in the light of these perceptions

flashback a sudden jump backwards in time to an earlier episode or incident. Stevens's narrative chronicles his drive from Darlington Hall to Cornwall in 1956; he breaks off from his account of the expedition, in a series of flashbacks, to refer to and describe various memories of his from 1923 to 1936

idiom a phrase or way of expressing something special to a language. Often the meaning of an idiomatic phrase, such as Mr Taylor's 'Hard to put your finger on it' (p. 194), cannot be predicted from the meanings of the words which make up the expression

Y

imagery in its narrowest sense an image is a picture in words – a description of some visible scene or object. More commonly, however, 'imagery' refers to the figurative language in a work of literature, such as metaphors and similes; or all the words which refer to objects and qualities which appeal to the senses and feelings

irony a use of language, widespread in all kinds of literature and everyday speech, which is characterised by saying or writing one thing while another is meant. The term 'irony' can also be used to describe an incongruity between what might be expected and what actually happens

literal language language which is used in a precise and limited sense, as opposed to more figurative uses of language, such as metaphor, which rely on words' associations and ambiguities to suggest something more than what is 'literally' meant

Marxist criticism Marxist critical theory, based on the economic, philosophical and political thinking of Karl Marx (1818–83), considers literature in relation to its capacity to reflect the struggle between the classes, and to reflect the economic conditions which are considered to lie at the heart of human intellectual and social evolution

metaphor derived from the Greek meaning 'carrying over', the term 'metaphor' describes a departure from literal writing which goes further than a comparison (or simile) between two different things or ideas by fusing them together: one thing is described as being another thing, thus 'carrying over' all its associations

motif a literary device, such as a theme, image or symbol, which recurs frequently, either within a body of literature or within a single work

narrative a story, tale or recital of a specific selection of events, constructed so as to suggest some relationship between them

narrator the person who tells the story. The narrator can be distinguished from the author of a work: in *The Remains of the Day*, although we know the novel to have been written by Kazuo Ishiguro, it is the character of Stevens who is the narrator, the fictional person who we choose to accept as having constructed the narrative

parody an imitation which ridicules the characteristic features of that which is being parodied

pathetic fallacy a term coined by John Ruskin to refer (pejoratively) to the attribution of human feelings to inanimate objects (a form of personification). Today the term is used, descriptively rather than negatively, to refer to the identification of a character's feelings with the properties of the external world: often this means equating mood and emotion to the weather and setting. Rain, for example, mirrors Stevens's heartbreak and the tragic tone of the conversation at the bus stop, just as fog connects to the lack of communication and understanding in the summerhouse

pathos a strong feeling of pity or sorrow. In *The Remains of the Day* pathos is evident, for example, when Stevens's father dies and when Stevens waits at the bus stop with Miss Kenton. It is also evident in less obvious incidents, such as when Stevens's father retraces his steps after his fall, seemingly searching for a lost jewel. Throughout the novel, the pathos is heightened by Stevens's sense of restraint and self-control within the narrative

post-structuralism a furthering of the linguistic theories of Ferdinand de Saussure, the Swiss linguist who developed the structuralist network of ideas. The most significant post-structuralist developments have been made by Roland Barthes, who analysed how meaning is produced by writing, and Jacques Derrida, who pioneered the linguistic philosophy of deconstruction

psychoanalytic criticism the application of theories of psychoanalysis (particularly those of Sigmund Freud) to literature in order to discover and analyse connections between writers and their work. Early psychoanalytic criticism involved attempts to 'read' the motivations of literary characters as if they were real people; by extension, literary characters were sometimes regarded as a means of access to the author's (presumed) psychological condition. More recent criticism, following the ideas of the French thinker Jacques Lacan, is concerned with the relationship between identity, language and desire

register a level of language associated with (and hence deemed appropriate to) a particular situation

satire literature which exhibits or examines vice and folly and makes them appear ridiculous or contemptible. Satire is directed against a person or a type, and is usually morally censorious, using laughter as a means of attack rather than merely for the evocation of mirth or pleasure

structuralism a theory begun by Ferdinand de Saussure, examining aspects of human society, including language and literature, where the parts only derive meaning from their place in the system they belong to. Words are seen to have an arbitrary relationship with the objects or feelings they describe

symbol something which represents something else by analogy or association – a writer may use conventional symbols, which form part of a literary or cultural tradition, as well as creating new ones

trope a word or phrase used in a sense not proper to it. In *The Remains of the Day* the story of the tiger under the table is a trope: Stevens's 'tiger under the table' is not literal, but a time when his dignity is put to the test

AUTHOR OF THIS NOTE

Sarah Peters is a teacher at an 11–18 comprehensive school in Newbury. She is second in the Department in charge of GCSE English and is a GCSE Examiner. She took her first degree at St David's University College, Lampeter, and is currently studying for an MA at Oxford Brookes University.

NOTES